Promoting Student Resiliency

Kris Bosworth
and
Garry R. Walz

Promoting Student Resiliency

10   9   8   7   6   5   4   3   2   1

American Counseling Association Foundation
5999 Stevenson Avenue
Alexandria, VA 22304

Cover design by Martha Woolsey.
Cover photograph by Garry R. Walz.

• • •

The choice of a cactus for the cover of this publication is a studied choice. We wanted the cover to mirror the essential message of the publication—that resilience is an essential characteristic for all persons in today's world. It is especially important in that it is a characteristic that can be managed by a person by him or herself. It is also an area of high criticality for counselors in their work with persons of all ages.

The cactus displayed on the cover is a healthy Arizona saguaro cactus. It, like all cacti, is noted for its ability to overcome extreme environmental deprivation (i.e., drought) for extended periods of time and still display both beauty and strength. Through careful internal management of its resources, it is able to offer a large and beautiful blossom. This ability parallels what the resilient person is able to do.

We hope you agree that a "cactus characteristic" is something we should all strive to acquire.

• • •

Library of Congress Cataloging-in-Publication Data
Bosworth, Kris.
  Promoting student resiliency / Kris Bosworth & Garry Walz.
      p. cm.
  Includes bibliographical references.
  ISBN 1-55620-263-6 (alk. paper)
  1. Educational counseling—United States. 2. Students—Psychology.
3. Resilience (Personality trait) I. Walz, Garry Richard. II. Title.

LB1027.5.B643 2005
371.4—dc22   2005005422

Table of Contents

Chapter 8
Resiliency in Action: Exemplary Models of Effective Practices and Programs *81*

References *95*

Preface

This publication is a product of discussions and collaboration over a period of time between the former ERIC/CASS Clearinghouse and the newly formed Counseling Outfitters, LLC, with American Counseling Association (ACA) Executive Director Richard Yep, American Counseling Association Foundation (ACAF) Chair Clemmie Solomon, and American Counseling Association Foundation (ACAF) Chair-Elect Jane Goodman.

ERIC/CASS had a long-standing interest in resiliency, self-efficacy, and self-esteem, having published several books and offered national workshops on the topic. That interest led us to Professor Kris Bosworth at the University of Arizona. Dr. Bosworth is known for both her scholarship and research as well as her direct field experience in school-based resiliency programs. Our discussions with her led to her leadership in writing this publication.

With the demise of the ERIC Clearinghouses, Counseling Outfitters, LLC, was formed by Garry Walz and Jeanne Bleuer to continue to offer the services and products for counselors and human services specialists that had been developed by ERIC/CASS, frequently in collaboration with ACA and ACAF.

Therefore, it only seemed proper that one of the first publications developed by Counseling Outfitters, LLC, should be done in collaboration with ACAF and mirror ACAF's continuing focus on empowering students. We hope this will be a forerunner of a continuing collaboration with ACAF to offer quality resources to counselors.

Garry R. Walz, Ph.D., NCC
Jeanne C. Bleuer, Ph.D., NCC

Introduction

Garry R. Walz

It is part of the American character to have a special appreciation for persons who overcome great odds to achieve something that was fervently desired but beyond a reasonable expectation of what was possible. Perhaps few events have so illustrated this characteristic as the victory of a young, untested American hockey team over an experienced, highly favored Russian team in the World Olympics. Subsequently made into a movie, the story has often been used as an example in sports as to how, if the will is strong enough, persons can overcome seemingly impossible obstacles. While savvy coaches perceive superior performance as much more than will, the story does illustrate how Americans applaud the underdog who comes from behind.

In a sense, this passion for overcoming obstacles and doing better than what was thought to be possible has been the subject of great discussion, speculation, and study in education. This focus has taken many forms, from fad to serious investigation. A broad self-esteem movement has strived to give students the message, "You can be and do whatever you believe you can." A more scholarly movement grounded in psychological research contends that, as performance improves, so does the belief in one's own abilities (self-efficacy). Both points of view have had their adherents in education and counseling. More recently, investigators working worldwide, but mostly independently of one another, have focused on the concept of resilience. As Dr. Bosworth explains in chapter 1, this term is applied to individuals who are able to "weather a storm in their lives, bounce back from adversity, or grow stronger in the face of adversity."

As a counselor educator and founder and director of the ERIC Clearinghouse on Counseling and Student Services, I have been intrigued by the potential potency of this concept for counselors in their work with clients of all ages and backgrounds. My own experience has been that counselors frequently encounter students who demonstrate successful coping skills and life outcomes in spite of backgrounds that would typically predict unfavorable outcomes such as dropping out, poor academic performance, or unsatisfactory social interactions. Usually, counselors are puzzled by why some clients or students exhibit this ability to overcome adversity, while others do not. Conversely, counselors almost routinely have clients or students who, despite significant "advantages" in background and family support, perform poorly, defying the conventional expectations that they would do well.

Sometimes referred to as "false negatives" (those who do better than expected) or "false positives" (those who do less well than expected), these students have posed difficult challenges to counselors because they do not fit well into the usual counseling theoretical approaches. When confronted by such students, counselors have resorted to "seat of the pants" interventions, using whatever approach seems to work even though they lack a logical or theoretical framework from which to work.

While counselors are certainly to be lauded for their personal resourcefulness in responding to the "resilience dilemma," the work of a large body of human development researchers has led to the identification of factors that can be nurtured in students in order to increase their ability to successfully cope with the challenges they encounter. It is my belief that the aforementioned body of research on resilience has been used infrequently by counselors in their counseling interventions and guidance curricula that led me to seek out Dr. Kris Bosworth, a research professor at the University of Arizona who has worked extensively on this topic for many years. Notably, her work has not been confined to the laboratory, but has involved several field investigations where she has led a large-scale program to implement the use of resilience promotion concepts by counselors, teachers, and administrators in actual school settings.

Dr. Bosworth graciously and enthusiastically responded to my invitation to collaborate on the development of a practical guide for counselors, educators, and administrators on the use of a resiliency orientation to counseling derived from a judicious use of resilience research. Her work, experience, and insights have demonstrated that very favorable outcomes can occur when a resiliency orientation to education and learning is utilized; and this is what has provided the driving force for this publication.

Starting at the End

Having taught effective reading and learning skills at the college level for many years, I acquired the habit of always reading the last chapter of a treatise first, be it a book, document, or scholarly paper. This approach enables me to see where the author is headed and greatly improves my comprehension of what he or she has to say when I return to read from the beginning. With a nod to "beginning at the end," I wish to share up front what I expect and hope you will acquire as you read and reflect on the ideas and suggestions offered in this book. It is not, as you can readily understand, a one-read book. You will want to examine and hopefully discuss with others what is presented. Ultimately, you can pick and choose what is attractive to you and adopt and adapt the material to your own counseling program and intervention style. What I reference here are only some of the exciting and compelling ideas and approaches that are presented in the book. They illustrate how a resilience orientation to counseling and education can make a real difference in student outcomes.

Idea Stimulators

1. *The ideas presented herein, although not always identified as such, can be put into two categories: counseling interventions and curriculum emphases.*

First are those ideas that are best suited for use in your individual or group counseling sessions. Second are those ideas which primarily lend themselves to an application to the guidance curriculum, or Comprehensive School Guidance Program, which has become the staple of many school guidance and counseling programs. As you read, consider where, when, and how you could apply the ideas presented. Clearly, not everyone will think the same way or make the same applications. Good! A resiliency-oriented counseling program is a good way to express your creativity.

2. *A resiliency orientation should be introduced early on in both counseling interventions and the guidance curriculum.*

The subject matter of counseling is typically about making choices and changes in one's life. Those choices and changes will reflect the sense of strength and confidence a person feels about him or herself. A resilient person is more likely to choose non-traditional careers or think outside the traditional box in making choices about his or her life and career plans. Students who have a resilience perspective that has been built on their knowledge of and appreciation for their personal strengths can make strong, but sometimes difficult, choices. In an excellent chapter in this book, Dr. Jane Goodman illustrates how resiliency impacts career development in varying situations.

3. *All persons are subjected to both risk factors and protective factors in their daily lives.*

An emphasis on the protective factors (those that prepare a person to better manage adversity) through a resiliency orientation can be useful to all students as well as faculty. Whereas the risk factors may more likely be the focus of individual or group counseling interventions, a focus on the protective factors through a schoolwide program can be of value to all students. The risk and protective factors that affect resiliency are fully discussed in chapter 1.

4. *Although the benefits of the No Child Left Behind legislation may be long debated, willy nilly, some children will be left behind.*
This is due to the fact that the risk factors discussed in this book have impeded many children's ability and motivation to learn. Although these risk factors have not been specifically identified in the legislation, attending to them may greatly enhance the learning progress of children in danger of being left behind.

5. *By creating a resiliency-oriented environment in a school, a buffer can be introduced against myriad risk factors.*
This buffer, formed by the overall impact of a resiliency orientation, will serve to protect students from risk factors that the schools cannot directly control. Very often, home and community conditions negatively affect students, and schools are not able to directly intervene. By strengthening the protective factors, students can be better prepared to deal with these conditions themselves.

6. *Through a counselor's leadership, there can be a shift in a school's focus from identifying problems to providing solutions.*
To do this will require that the counselor assume a schoolwide leadership role that involves participation by many, if not all, faculty. It means moving from a focus on labeling to a focus on bringing about positive outcomes.

7. *The counselor can play an important role in stressing that a strong "self-righting" phenomenon exists with regard to students.*
Most students can overcome difficult backgrounds and circumstances, particularly if others express their belief in them. Premature and permanent labeling of students is at variance with the research that shows that most overcome bad backgrounds and go on to live successful lives.

Some Concluding Observations

In a recent publication entitled, *Knowledge Nomads and the Nervously Employed: Workplace Change and Courageous Career Choices* (Feller & Whichard, 2005), the challenges facing children and adults today are graphically and dramatically portrayed. According to the authors, to cope with the challenges that our society is imposing on persons today, individuals need to be continually involved in making courageous choices with regard to their careers and lives. As suggested earlier, it is the person who knows and acts on his or her strengths who can most readily make the courageous choices that successful school and life outcomes require.

In *Unfocused Kids: Helping Students to Focus on Their Education and Career Plans* (Wakefield, Sage, Coy, & Palmer, 2004), Suzy Mygatt Wakefield, a lifelong school counselor, describes the large and expanding group of students who are unable to focus on life or career plans while in school and leave school early unprepared for working and living in today's world. In a sense, they have been overwhelmed by risk factors, and neither they themselves nor the schools have been able to provide the protective factors they need to meet unexpected challenges and make necessary changes in their behaviors.

Hopefully, as you read on, you will gain insight into the need to build a resiliency orientation into your counseling program and will be able to identify specific guidance program or counseling interventions that you can employ. It is a challenging, but potentially very rewarding, opportunity. I believe that it is particularly compelling that each counselor can choose from a wide array of options those that can make his or her own counseling more resiliency-oriented.

About the Authors

Kris Bosworth, Ph.D., is the Smith Endowed Chair in Substance Abuse Education and a professor in the College of Education at the University of Arizona. She currently serves as the head of the Educational Leadership Program and is a member of the Tucson Resiliency Initiative. She holds a master's in Counseling and Guidance (1975) and a Ph.D. (1988) in Adult Education (Program Evaluation and Educational Technology) from the University of Wisconsin-Madison. Her most recent work (*Protective Schools*) has focused on creating and maintaining school and classroom climates that are protective and support resiliency.

Garry R. Walz, Ph.D., NCC, established and directed the ERIC Counseling and Student Services Clearinghouse at the University of North Carolina at Greensboro. He started the clearinghouse at the University of Michigan in 1966 and served as its director until 1993, when it moved to North Carolina. He is also a Professor Emeritus of the University of Michigan.

Dr. Walz has authored and co-authored numerous books and articles and initiated and directed the ERIC/CASS Virtual Libraries.

He is a past president of the American Counseling Association and the Association for Counselor Education and Supervision, as well as a past chair of the Counseling and Human Development Foundation. He has been recognized with the ACA Gilbert and Kathleen Wrenn Humanitarian Award and the National Career Development Association's Eminent Professional Career Award.

Chapter 1

Overview of Resiliency

Resilient is a term used in the physical sciences to describe substances that have the ability to return to their original form after being bent, compressed, or stretched. Applied to individuals, the term is used to describe people who are able to weather a storm in their lives, bounce back from adversity, or grow stronger in the face of adversity. It is often used to describe students who succeed in spite of adverse family, socioeconomic, or other high-stress environmental conditions.

Beginning in the late 1970s with the landmark studies of Werner and Smith (1982) and Rutter, Maughan, Martimore, and Ouston (1979), researchers began to investigate why some children experienced positive life outcomes in spite of less-than-optimal backgrounds or circumstances that would typically predict developmental failure. They used the term *resiliency* to describe these children's capacity to overcome adversity and identified several factors at the levels of the individual, family, and environment that contribute to resiliency in children. Some factors, such as birth order, are not amenable to change. There are, however, other factors that caring adults can deliberately promote in order to increase children's ability to overcome whatever challenges they face in their lives. Examples are ensuring the presence of caring, supportive adults who believe in the child; teaching the child skills for seeking help or support from adults; and affirming a positive attitude that life holds promise and that the child has the skills to succeed in life.

Risk and Protective Factors

The following two brief case examples illustrate opposing myths about youths who experience adversity in their lives. Their stories, and the assumptions drawn about their lives, are reflective of thousands of other young people around the country. They illustrate a paradigm that provides an important foundation for resiliency research: namely, that factors exist that either increase or reduce a young person's ability to cope with the challenges of life.

Michael's Story

> *Michael, a ninth grader, is facing possible expulsion for having brought a knife to school. At his expulsion hearing, the school social worker describes Michael's home as chaotic. The family has moved at least a dozen times since Michael has been in school. The father is an alcoholic, and the mother is overwhelmed by the responsibility of taking care of five children, the eldest of which is Michael. The father is a construction worker, and when he is able to work, he makes good money. However, his bouts of drinking and the seasonal nature of construction work mean that the family regularly experiences periods of poverty.*
>
> *Michael, who is small for his age, has been diagnosed with a learning disability and has been receiving special education resource services since the fourth grade. Because of the family's frequent moves, however, his education has often been interrupted. Because of his small size, Michael often feels he must defend himself. As a result, he has been involved in numerous fights, beginning in the elementary grades.*

All school counselors are familiar with students like Michael, who are regularly referred to the counselor's office for either behavioral or academic concerns. Given repeated experiences with students like these, many counselors may come to believe that students from high-stress and unstable backgrounds are inevitably launched on a trajectory toward failure in school and life. As the next case study shows, however, these troubled students may be in the minority and may simply be the most visible segment of students living in high-stress environments.

Jenny's Story

> *When Jenny was seven, her parents divorced. At that time, her mother had just been diagnosed with clinical depression, and her father had just been arrested*

for the third time for possession of illegal substances. When Jenny was nine, her mother married a successful business owner who was an alcoholic. Her mother's depression worsened, and by the time Jenny graduated from high school, her mother spent most days in bed watching television.

Jenny was born with an engaging personality and above-average intelligence. Early in her school career, teachers encouraged Jenny to use her intelligence, offered her support and positive feedback, and challenged her academically. Jenny thrived within the public school system, despite continual turbulence, chaos, and neglect at home.

Counselors also have seen hundreds of children like Jenny, who come from disadvantaged backgrounds and yet are able to succeed where many would predict failure for them. In many ways, Jenny exemplifies the myth of the golden child—the belief that personal fortitude can surmount adversity and that people can pull themselves up by their own bootstraps.

In reality, Jenny's success resulted not from any magical or "golden" qualities, but from a number of factors that provided her with attitudes and skills that opened up alternatives to forge a successful life. Studies of young people like Jenny, who achieve success despite an adverse or high-stress background, have given the counseling profession a fresh perspective on providing situations and environments that are conducive to building the skills necessary to be successful in spite of the challenges in one's background.

Risk factors are personal, familial, or environmental characteristics that predispose a person to a negative developmental outcome. Psychologist Mark Katz (1997) describes risk factors as those events, experiences, or conditions that increase the chance that a person will have problems. The preceding case studies exemplify multiple risk factors: family alcoholism and depression, overstressed and neglectful parents, lack of bonding to school because of frequent moves, and early predisposition to violence. Yet, there were also other conditions of Michael's and Jenny's environments that influenced the dramatically different directions their lives took. These conditions are known as *protective factors*, factors that buffer against, or mediate, the risk of developmental failure. In Jenny's case, her personality, intelligence, and bonding to teachers and school served as protective factors that helped her to have a much more successful outcome.

David Hawkins and his colleagues at the University of Washington (Hawkins, Catalano, & Miller, 1992) reviewed hundreds of studies of young people who use alcohol, tobacco, and other drugs. They identified risk factors that recurred in numerous studies spanning a period of 30 years or more. Among the risk factors they identified are influences in many domains:

Community Factors
    1. Laws and norms favorable toward risk-taking behavior
    2. Availability of the substance of abuse
    3. Extreme economic deprivation
    4. Neighborhood disorganization

Family Factors
    5. Family behavior and attitudes regarding alcohol and drugs
    6. Poor and inconsistent family management practices
    7. Family conflict
    8. Low bonding to family

School Factors
    9. Early and persistent problem behavior
    10. Academic failure
    11. Low degree of commitment to school

Individual/Peer Factors
    12. Peer rejection in elementary grades
    13. Association with drug-using peers
    14. Alienation and rebelliousness
    15. Attitudes favorable to drug use
    16. Early onset of drug use

Although these risk factors are specific to the development of substance abuse, most also appear to contribute to other negative outcomes, such as school failure, dropping out, pregnancy, and delinquency. Notice that these risk factors are drawn from many different domains, including characteristics of the individual, the family or school environment, and relationships with peer groups and the broader community, as well as legal, economic, and cultural factors (Hawkins, et al., 1992).

Considerably fewer studies explore protective factors that can mediate or moderate the effects of exposure to risk. However, Hawkins and colleagues (1992) have identified certain protective factors, including these:

1. Strong attachment, or bonding, between parent and teenager
2. Parents' support of conventional norms
3. The child's temperament
4. Family support
5. External support system that encourages and reinforces the child's efforts to cope (e.g., adults who act as mentors and role models)
6. The child's repertoire of social problem-solving skills
7. The child's belief in his or her self-efficacy and ability to succeed

Another approach to the study of risk and protective factors comes from the work of the Search Institute (Scales & Leffort, 1999). Since the late 1980s, the Search Institute has been surveying sixth to twelfth graders in more than 600 communities across the country (Benson, 1997). Their quest was to identify those developmental assets, or building blocks, that all youth need to grow into healthy, caring, principled, and productive adults. Based on a sample of nearly 100,000 students gathered during the 1996–97 school year, Search Institute researchers found that the number of assets a student had was inversely related to risk-taking behavior in many domains, including alcohol, tobacco, illicit drugs, early sexual intercourse, depression, suicide, antisocial behavior, violence, school problems, driving under the influence, and gambling. Simultaneously, a high number of assets correlated with student reports of a large number of positive behaviors, such as succeeding in school, helping others, valuing diversity, maintaining good health, exhibiting leadership skills, resisting danger, delaying gratification, and overcoming adversity. In addition, the effect of protective factors (assets) was more powerful for youth in high-risk situations than for other youth, a finding consistent with several other studies. Table 1.1 lists the 40 developmental assets identified by the Search Institute.

Vulnerability and Resiliency

Having outlined the risk and protective factors paradigm, we can return to the concept of resiliency, and its flip side, *vulnerability*. Whereas resiliency is the ability to withstand or surmount risk, vulnerability implies an intensified susceptibility to risk. Rutter and colleagues (1979) have suggested that protective processes and variables operate synergistically to create a shield of resilience against the risk for negative outcomes created by the presence of risk factors.

How does this interaction between risk and protective factors play out over time? What evidence do we have that protective factors can actually change the trajectory of a young person's life? Two studies are important in answering these questions. In 1955, Emmy Werner

Table 1.1 Forty Developmental Assets

	ASSET TYPE	ASSET NAME & DEFINITION
EXTERNAL ASSETS	Support	1. Family support 2. Positive family communication 3. Other adult relationships 4. Caring neighborhood 5. Caring school climate 6. Parent involvement in schooling
	Empowerment	7. Community that values youth 8. Youth as resources 9. Service to others 10. Safety
	Boundaries and expectations	11. Family boundaries 12. School boundaries 13. Neighborhood boundaries 14. Adult role models 15. Positive peer influences 16. High expectations
	Constructive use of time	17. Creative activities 18. Youth program 19. Religious community 20. Time at home
INTERNAL ASSETS	Commitment to learning	21. Achievement motivation 22. School engagement 23. Homework 24. Bonding to school 25. Reading for pleasure
	Positive values	26. Caring 27. Equality and social justice 28. Integrity

Table 1.1 (continued)

		29. Honesty 30. Responsibility 31. Restraint
	Social competencies	32. Planning and decision making 33. Interpersonal competence 34. Cultural competence 35. Resistance skills 36. Peaceful conflict resolution
	Positive identity	37. Personal power 38. Self-esteem 39. Sense of purpose 40. Positive view of personal future

Source: Scales, P. C., & Leffort, N. (1999). *Developmental assets: A synthesis of the scientific research on adolescent development.* Minneapolis, MN: Search Institute.

and Ruth Smith began collecting data on all children born in that year on the island of Kauai, Hawaii. At the time of the study, Kauai had not been discovered as a holiday paradise, but was an important location for the pineapple and sugarcane industries. Waves of foreign workers were brought to the island to work in these industries, so that by 1955, the island was quite multicultural. Of the children studied, 33% were Japanese, 23% Hawaiian, 17% Filipino, 6% Portuguese, 3% Anglo Saxon Caucasian, and 17% of mixed or other ethnicity, including Chinese, Korean, and Puerto Rican. The island was characterized by high rates of poverty and alcoholism.

This group of children has been followed periodically since the baseline data were collected in 1955. Over the years, Werner and Smith have taken extensive measures of health, educational, social, and emotional factors (1982, 1992, 2001). Werner and Smith focused some of their research on the most vulnerable group of these 1955 babies: those children who at birth had four or more identified risk factors. Among these factors were difficulty with the mother's pregnancy or delivery, birth defects, poverty, alcoholism, mental illness, and absence of a parent. About 270 of the 614 babies fell into this category and have formed the cohort sample. The study of these children has made an important contribution to understanding the interplay between risk and protective factors.

At age 18, more than a third of those children with high levels of risk were doing well in many ways . They were making progress in school and had avoided delinquency or teen pregnancy. They also reported feelings of well-being (Werner & Smith, 1982). When surveyed again at age 32, a surprising 67% of the high-risk cohort reported positive outcomes, including positive self-reports on mental health indicators (Werner & Smith, 1992). By the time they were 40, 60% of the men and 70% of the women felt satisfied with their lives (Werner & Smith, 2001).

Werner and Smith described this phenomenon as "the self-righting tendencies in human nature and the capacity of *most* individuals who grow up in adverse circumstances to make a successful adaptation in adulthood" (Werner & Smith, 2001, p. 166). Like Hawkins, Catalano, and Miller (1992) and the Search Institute (Scales & Leffort, 1999), Werner and Smith found protective factors in several domains, including individual, family, school, and community. Key indicators were the following:

1. A temperament in the child that elicited positive responses from caregivers.
2. Problem-solving skill in middle childhood.
3. A fairly small number of children in the family (four or fewer).
4. Presence of caregivers other than the parents.
5. Structure and rules in the household during adolescence.

Also critical were supportive teachers in the school who acted as role models and who assisted in developing and supporting realistic educational and vocational plans. The opening of opportunities increased the youngsters' competence and confidence. Three strong clusters of protective factors differentiate the resilient group from those high-risk youth who developed serious and recurring problems in childhood and adolescence:

1. Disposition and attitudes that elicited positive responses from family members and acquaintances, including robustness, vigor, and active, sociable temperament.
2. Affectional ties with parent substitutes, such as grandparents, older siblings, and teachers, who encouraged trust, autonomy, and initiative.
3. An external support system through church, youth groups,

or school that rewarded competence and provided a sense of stability.

Although most of the children from adverse backgrounds did well in adulthood, some did not. On the positive side, most delinquent youth in this group did not go on to an adult criminal career. Only 25% of the males and 10% of the females who committed juvenile offenses had criminal records by age 32. However, those individuals with adult criminal records also reported other negative outcomes such as broken marriages, family violence, and employment difficulties. These findings are similar to those from other studies with very different populations. For example, Farrington (1989), who studied males in the mid-1950s, also found that early delinquency is not an automatic path to adult criminal activity.

Based on their research and that of others, Werner and Smith (1982, 1992) concluded that protective factors, or buffers, have a more profound impact on the life course of children who grow up in adverse conditions than do specific risk factors or stressful life events. The buffers appear to transcend ethnicity, social class, and geographic and historical boundaries. Werner and Smith's longitudinal research offers an optimistic perspective on the consequences of growing up in adverse conditions and repeatedly highlights "self-righting" tendencies, which educators can use to shape environments and interventions that will support normal, healthy development for all human beings.

A common theme that runs throughout these studies is the role that a caring adult can play in the life of a child through providing consistency, stability, and unconditional love and support. As philosopher and educator Nel Noddings (1992) states, "The desire to be cared for is almost certainly a universal human characteristic" (p. 17). For children and youth who do not experience caring in any other environment, schools may become the only place they see caring adult relationships practiced and modeled. Counselors and other educators have the opportunity to play powerful roles in the lives of children that extend beyond academic content and the curriculum. If students cannot find these models somewhere in their lives, their academic and social growth will likely suffer.

In the next chapter, we move on to present statistics on the numbers of adolescents who are engaging in high-risk behaviors such as alcohol, tobacco, and other drug use; violence; sexual activity; and thoughts of or attempts at suicide. Given that these youth represent our future social capital, there are alarming indications that the United States will continue to be one of the countries with the highest rates of these behaviors in the developed world.

Counselors play a key role in setting the tone of the school. On a daily basis, they are models for positive communication and provide support for students, as well as staff and families. They have the flexibility to teach skills that will support the creation and maintenance of a protective climate in the school.

Chapter 2

The Facts and Figures on Teen Risk-Taking Behaviors

In their first two decades of life, American youth face numerous challenges and choices about lifestyle and health. Changes in family structure, the prevalence of media influences, and an increase in family mobility have weakened traditional family and social bonds, thus increasing the importance of educators in directly teaching about lifestyle choices, as well as modeling appropriate behavior and creating environments where students at all levels can practice positive social skills. Risk-taking behaviors such as the use of tobacco, alcohol, and other drugs; sexual activity; gang involvement; and violence have permeated public schools. In response, health professionals and politicians have called on schools to act as sites for prevention and intervention. Although educators have frequently questioned what the role of schools should be in addressing student issues outside the realm of academics, risk behaviors may directly interfere with learning, in addition to being a threat to physical and mental health, making it difficult for schools to ignore them.

Statistics on adolescent risk-taking behaviors can be found in a number of scientifically valid studies conducted over the course of many years. The Monitoring the Future Study, which began collecting annual data on youth drug use in the 1970s, has become one of the most reliable sources of data for analyzing trends and patterns of drug use (www.monitoringthefuture.org). More recently, the Centers for Disease Control and Prevention (CDC) has begun the Youth Risk Behavior Surveillance System (YRBSS), collecting data biannually on a range of risk behaviors of school-going youth (http://www.cdc.gov/HealthyYouth/yrbs). A still more comprehensive survey is the National Survey on Drug Use & Health (formerly referred to as the National Household Survey on Drug Abuse; http://samhsa.gov). Adolescents form a subset of an annual telephone survey of the general population. Data from this study provide information on teens who are not attending school.

Drugs, Alcohol, and Tobacco

Although statistics in the 2001 National Household Survey on Drug Abuse (NHSDA) show a general overall decline in teen alcohol and tobacco use (the most commonly used drugs by teens) since 1996, the rate of adolescent experimentation with illegal drugs, alcohol, and tobacco remains alarmingly high. Moreover, some of the more dangerous drugs, such as ecstasy, are showing increased levels of adolescent usage (Substance Abuse and Mental Health Services Administration [SAMSHA], 2002).

According to the 2003 Monitoring the Future Study, which sampled 44,000 students between eighth and twelfth grades; 20% of eighth, 36% of tenth, and 49% of twelfth graders had consumed alcohol in the past 30 days during 2002. This means that in classes of 30 students at these grades, an average of 6 eighth graders, 11 sophomores, and 15 seniors will have consumed alcohol in the previous 30 days. Considering that alcoholics report earlier and higher levels of usage of alcohol during adolescence than nonalcoholic adults, attempts at intervention should be targeted at this population (Johnston, O'Malley, & Bachman, 2003).

From 1990 to 1996, the incidence rate of new marijuana users climbed steadily from 1.4 million per year to 2.5 million per year. Between 1996 and 2001, the number of new users per year held constant at around 2.5 million, with the average age of initiation being 17.5 years (CDC, 2001). In the 2001 YRBSS, 23.9% of high school–age students self-reported smoking marijuana in the previous 30 days, with 5.4% reporting smoking marijuana on school grounds in the past 30 days. This means that in a typical high school class of 30 students, seven would have smoked marijuana, and two would have smoked marijuana on campus in the previous 30 days.

Cocaine usage has generally increased between 1986 and 2000. In 1986 the incidence rate of cocaine use was 300,000 per year; by 2000, this rate had increased to 360,000 per year (SAMSHA, 2002). As of 2001 it is estimated that 9.4% of high school students have tried cocaine once in their lifetime and that 4.2% have used cocaine in the past 30 days (CDC, 2001).

Student use of hallucinogenic drugs, such as MDMA (ecstasy), LSD (acid), and psilocybin (mushrooms), have increased markedly since 1990. In 1990, there were approximately 600,000 new users, whereas in 2000 nearly 1.5 million individuals reported using some form of hallucinogenic drug for the first time. This is a tripling of the initiation rate in a 10-year period (SAMSHA, 2002). It is estimated that in 2001, 6.2% of 10th graders and 9.2% of 12th graders nationwide experimented with ecstasy (Johnston et al., 2003). This increase in the usage of ecstasy is very startling from a public health point of view because of the unknown potential interactions and side effects of the drug, which have led to several highly publicized and unnecessary deaths of adolescents (Goldberg, Frost-Pineda, & Gold, 2002).

Tobacco usage by adolescents declined from 1999 to 2000, from 2 million new users per year to 1.6 million new users per year. Although there has been a general decline in tobacco usage since 1996, in 2001 33.9% of America's high school–aged youth still reported having smoked a cigarette in the past 30 days (SAMSHA, 2002). Another study reports that 63.9% of teenagers reported having taken at least one puff from a cigarette in their lifetime. The highly addictive nature of cigarettes is demonstrated in self-reports of current adolescent smokers: 57.4% of them report having tried to quit smoking in the past 12 months. Of additional concern is the fact that many adolescents falsely perceive smokeless tobacco products to be a safer alternative to smoking. In 2000, 8.2% of adolescents reported having used smokeless tobacco in the past 30 days, with 5% of the student population admitting to having used smokeless tobacco on campus during the same time period (CDC, 2001).

Clearly, substance use has a dramatic effect on the lives of teens and their families. Judy Bowers, director of counseling for the Tucson Unified School District, said, "Kids cannot be successful in school if they are high on drugs. I see drug use (including alcohol) as the number-one cause of absences, tardiness, and academic underachievement in school" (J. Bowers, personal communication, 2000). Research indicates that adolescents who abuse alcohol may remember 10% less of what they learn than those who do not drink (Grant & Dawson, 1997).

Sexual Activity

Premature sexual activity by teenagers in the United States has both health and emotional risks. Of teenagers 15 to 17 years of age, 56% report having been with someone in a sexually intimate way. Among teenagers who have had sexual intercourse, 37% report having first intercourse before the age of 15 (Kaiser Family Foundation, 2003). Of the teenagers who reported having had sexual intercourse in the past 30 days, 42% did not use a condom (CDC, 2001). Out of a total of 12 million individuals newly infected with an STD each year, 3 million are teenagers. Several of these diseases have life-altering effects:

chlamydia may result in future sterility; syphilis may cause blindness and, for women during pregnancy, maternal death and death of the infant; and HIV infection is fatal (Alan Guttmacher Institute, 1999). The United States also has the highest teen birth rate in the Western world. The National Center for Health Statistics, a division of the CDC, estimates that 1 million teenage girls become pregnant per year, with about 485,000 of them carrying the child to term (Ventura, Mosher, Curtin, Abma, & Henshaw, 1999). This means that around 2,740 teenage girls are being impregnated on a daily basis.

Violence

In spite of high profile school violence such as Columbine, the United States' youth homicide rates are the highest among the Western nations. Although the rates have decreased since the mid 1990s, violence is a major concern. Although schools, even to this day, remain the safest places for children to be in terms of mortality and morbidity, huge concern about the safety of students has rippled through almost every American community. In response, numerous programs, processes, and procedures were put in place to deal with conflict and violence (CDC, 2000).

Suicide

According to the 2001 Youth Risk Behavior Surveillance System Survey, suicide is the third leading cause of death among youths ages 15 to 24, accounting for 12% of all deaths in this age group. YRBSS data from 2001 show that 8.3% of students in Grades 9 through 12 had made a suicide attempt in the previous year, and 19.3% had seriously considered attempting suicide (CDC, 2001). When considered in relation to a high school with a student body of 2,000, these proportions would translate into 166 students making a suicide attempt each year, and 386 students contemplating suicide. Fortunately most of these students are unsuccessful in their attempts or decide not to attempt suicide, but as the statistics show, a large number are successful, either intentionally or accidentally.

Dropping Out

The National Center for Education Statistics (NCES) measures high school dropout rates by calculating the proportion of young adults between the ages of 16 and 24 who are not enrolled in a high school program and who have not received a high school diploma. Nationwide dropout rates have shown a general downward trend since 1972, when 14.6% of the eligible population dropped out of high school. In 2001, 10.7% of the eligible population had dropped out of high school. When this overall rate is disaggregated by race, disturbing racial disparities emerge. For White non-Hispanic students, the dropout rate is 7.3%; for African Americans, it is10.9%; and for Hispanics, the rate climbs to a shocking 27% (NCES, 2003). The costs of this disproportionate dropout rate in lost economic activity, quality of life, and social justice are difficult to estimate.

Relationship of Risk-Taking Behaviors to Resiliency

The National Longitudinal Study of Adolescent Health (Bearman, Jones, & Udry, 1997) surveyed more than 90,000 adolescents in Grades 7 through 12 in 80 different communities across the United States. The study indicated that schools where students report that they feel cared for by the people at their school and feel part of the school culture can be protective environments for students. Students in this kind of school culture are less likely to engage in unhealthy behavior such as substance abuse, premature sexual activity, and violent or deviant behavior.

Researchers found that 31% of the students sampled did not feel such a connection to school, and that these students were more likely to smoke cigarettes, have early sexual intercourse, or become involved in weapon-related violence. Not only does school connectedness buffer students against engaging in many health risk behaviors, it plays a role in supporting academic success as well (Blum, McNeely, & Rinehart, 2002).

School Counselor's Role in Helping Students Avoid Risk-Taking Behaviors

School counselors are often asked to take a leadership role in providing materials, instruction, programs, and other resources to prevent and combat risk-taking behaviors and negative lifestyle choices. They are also are called upon to deliver responsive remedial services to those who have already initiated these activities. As we discuss in Chapter 5, a comprehensive school counseling program can provide the framework for counselors to deliver these services.

Chapter 3

Resiliency and Academic Achievement

The educational landscape has changed dramatically over the past ten years. Through the No Child Left Behind Act, federal legislation and educational policy have driven an emphasis on accountability as measured by student achievement. In fact, raising student achievement has become the primary focus of school reform. With state and federal dollars increasingly being attached to test results, and students' futures increasingly dependent on how they perform on high-stakes testing, educational leaders are examining how each member of the school community, including the school counselor, can contribute to student academic success. Within the public school setting at all levels, student achievement has become part of the role of every adult in the school. To ensure that no child *is* left behind, schools must offer programs and interventions that span student needs on a continuum from normal developmental needs to crisis intervention. This means that school counselors need to examine their role within the school to determine how their expertise can support the academic mission of the school.

The premise behind many of the educational reforms is that either the structure of schools or the quality of instruction is the key to academic success. Yet at the same time, students are experiencing numerous barriers to learning that must be addressed before they can achieve academically. Some of the barriers—such as poverty, family discord, mental illness, alcohol or other drug abuse, or child abuse or neglect—usually require resources beyond a school's reach to resolve. Other barriers—such as lack of motivation, role models, educational goals, or confidence—are ones that can be addressed in a resiliency-oriented environment. Such an environment can buffer a student from the other risk factors that school personnel are unable to address directly. Thus, the programs and strategies that are consistent with a resiliency focus are essential to removing barriers to learning.

Removing Barriers to Learning

Many barriers to learning (such as poverty) may seem beyond the control of school personnel. As has been discussed in earlier chapters, however, a resiliency focus with attention to a positive school climate can buffer students from high-stress environments and provide support for academic success. A team of researchers from Howard University and Johns Hopkins University examined predictors of academic success for poor and minority students (Borman & Rachuba, 2001). Their sample included 925 poor and ethnically diverse students in the third grade. They found the strongest predictor of academic success among these students was student engagement in learning, followed by locus of control, self-efficacy in math, positive attitude toward school, and self-esteem. The authors concluded that "the most powerful models for promoting [academic] resiliency appear to be those elements that actively shield children from adversity" (p. 20). In addition, they report, "We find that attentiveness to the psychosocial adjustment and school engagement of academically at-risk students are the keys to academic resilience" (p. 21).

All the educators working within a school play critical roles in supporting academic success for all students by removing barriers to learning. According to the Metropolitan Life Foundation National School Counselor Training Initiative (Martin, 2002), school counselors are ideally positioned within a school to help remove the barriers to learning that many children face. On the other hand, a school counselor cannot be all things to all people. Based on the school's needs and the counselor's training and experience, his or her role has to be carefully defined and the time spent in a variety of activities carefully monitored. Initiating, organizing, and supporting schoolwide interventions may be more effective than intervening with individual children only.

Howard Adelman and Linda Taylor at the University of California, Los Angeles, have proposed an organizational model that can guide counselors in identifying their role in helping students overcome barriers to learning (Taylor & Adelman, 2000). They have identified three systems that interact in a school that work positively to remove or reduce the impact of barriers to learning.

The *management component* encompasses government oversight and resource management including the school facilities, transportation and maintenance systems, food service, administration of federal and state mandates and programs, and the instructional leadership in a school and district. As Rutter and colleagues (1979) noted, schools with relatively high achievement were more likely than other schools to be clean, neat, orderly, and well run. While strength in this component is necessary for achievement, it is not sufficient: A well-run school without strong instructional and enabling components is not likely to have high achievement.

The *instructional component* focuses on teaching methods, curriculum, and enrichment activities that are designed to facilitate learning. Teaching that is both engaging and interactive as well as based on sound theory and research is critical to the academic success of students. In the past 20 years, educational research has identified strategies and curricula that facilitate learning. Educators need to be aware of the research and select methods and content based on both an understanding of the needs of students and the research on methods and curricula.

The *enabling component* creates a school climate that fosters resiliency and development in students of the protective factors discussed in Chapter 1. The enabling component recognizes that not all students come to school motivationally ready and able to learn. Many students come to well-managed schools with fine instructional programs but are unmotivated or inadequately prepared to learn. Barriers within the enabling component involve a number of factors that often fall within the school counselor's or school social worker's realm, including poverty, mental or physical illness, dysfunctional family environment, alcohol or other drug abuse, and child neglect or abuse. Most of these barriers are environmental and beyond the power of an individual child to change. Many programs within schools, such as Head Start, free breakfast and lunch programs, and provision of medical screenings and services, exist out of a recognition that students whose basic needs are unmet cannot perform to the best of their ability.

Counselors may play important roles in recognizing when such problems exist, connecting the family with appropriate social services in the community or school and building capacity within the school and community. Yet, unfortunately, educators have limited ability to affect these issues on a large scale. The power educators do have is to make broad and powerful changes within the environment in the school.

In this three-component model, the counselor does not work alone to overcome the barriers to learning. Removing or reducing the barriers to learning requires teamwork and collaboration with the entire school staff. Studies of resiliency have identified several approaches to removing barriers to learning, including such things as creating a positive climate, setting and maintaining clear and consistent boundaries, setting high expectations, teaching social skills, and providing care and concern. The school counselor plays a major leadership role in these activities. This role is supported by the Education Trust's definition of school counseling as "a profession that focuses on the relations and interactions between students and their school environment with the expressed purpose of reducing the effect of environmental and institutional barriers to learning" (Martin, 2002).

Efforts to eliminate or reduce barriers to learning by creating protective school environments often involve a series of steps. For smooth implementation of such programs or strategies, the relationship between the counselor and the principal is critical. (See Chapter 7 for discussion of the implementation process.) As the complexity of the educational tasks within a school increases, leadership increasingly becomes a shared responsibility. Clearly leadership begins with the principal, but other key stakeholders, especially counselors, must take active leadership roles (National Association of Secondary School Principals, 1996).

Stone and Clark (2001) have identified five areas in which the principal and counselor can partner to promote academic success. Although the authors never specifically address creating positive, protective environments to remove the barriers to learning, each one of the suggestions supports the resiliency approach. Creating protective (resiliency-based) school environments is an essential ingredient to removing the barriers to learning.

1. *Changing beliefs and attitudes.* Counselors are human behavior and relations experts who can work with principals to influence staff attitudes about each student's abilities and to improve instruction and classroom management.
2. *Developing high expectations that children will achieve.* With principal support, counselors can take an active role in academic advising, as well as working individually and collectively with teachers to help them implement academically rigorous, evidence-based curricula.
3. *Changing course enrollment.* At the secondary school level, counselors can help students select courses and career planning efforts consistent with their career aspirations, ensuring that every student has the broadest possible range of educational opportunities.
4. *Conducting data analysis.* Effective decision -making is based on appropriate data that have been accurately collected and analyzed. Through the collection and analysis of data, the team of principal and counselor can identify systemic practices that are inequitable, as well as manage and monitor patterns of enrollment and student success.

5. *Providing staff development.* Counselors are in an ideal position to organize and deliver staff development to large groups of faculty. Because they interact with faculty on a regular basis, they also have opportunities to provide mentoring and coaching to faculty members, either individually or in groups.

Specific guidance for implementing strategies to remove barriers to learning and create an enabling environment is presented in Chapter 6. Meanwhile, the next chapter changes direction somewhat to focus on career preparation.

Chapter 4

Resiliency and Career Planning and Development

Jane Goodman

Joe Palooka was a comic strip boxer who debuted in 1930. In the 1950s, he became the hero of a television show. When I was a child, I owned an almost life-size blow-up doll of Joe Palooka. With a sand-weighted bottom, its design was such that when you knocked it over, it popped back up, presumably the way the character of Joe Palooka did in the ring. I have always maintained that image of resiliency. You may be knocked down, but you don't stay down!

Career resiliency has become a necessity in today's world of work. It has become a cliché that the average person will make — of choice or necessity — seven major career shifts during a working life (L. Peterson, 1995; Bureau of Labor Statistics, 1998). Chatzky (2003) estimated that each person will have 12 jobs during a working life. Yet it seems that many school-based career development programs focus on job choice rather than on transition skills. Although the initial job choice is clearly important, it is increasingly evident that the ability to manage a number of transitions is equally important. Managing transitions successfully is certainly dependent on resiliency.

In addition, focusing on choice as a unitary phenomenon sends the message that one choice will be enough. Thus children, and adults, are often unprepared when —not if — they are faced with unanticipated career transitions. On the other hand, many people find it a relief to know that their career decision making is one involving their first or next choice, not their only choice. Young people often react very negatively to the idea that they must choose, as they see it, a job they will have for life. Not only is this understandable psychologically, but, as we have said earlier, it is correct structurally. It is both unreasonable to expect that kind of decision with such long term effects from an adolescent and inaccurate to portray the world of work in those terms.

Several writers have discussed career resiliency in a broader context. For example, London (1998) saw resiliency, insight, and identity as part of career motivation, and included the concept of hardiness as part of the picture. *Hardiness*, often used as a synonym for or in conjunction with resiliency, connotes endurance or stamina. Resiliency as a concept includes hardiness, but goes further, to connote the buoyancy of recovery to one's original position.

Collard, Epperheimer, and Saign (1996), among many others, stated that the need for career resiliency is a result of the shift in the unspoken agreement between employer and employee in recent years. The earlier agreement of two-way loyalty has changed to one where each party is responsible for his or her well-being. Organizations need to focus on profit for stockholders; individuals need to focus on their own needs and be in charge of their own career development. Individual responsibility of this kind has come to be known as "You, Inc." An interesting example of this change comes from Michigan, where the telephone company, seen as a surrogate parent, was known fondly as "Ma Bell," a sobriquet it quickly lost during the layoffs of the 1980s.

Stevens (2001) argued that career resiliency education not only teaches employees career management skills but also reduces anxiety about change. Others, for example Grzeda (1999) and Griffith (1998), suggest that employers benefit from employees' career resiliency. An employee who wishes to be career resilient will, for example, take advantage of education and training opportunities. This clearly benefits the employer. Employers who used to worry about well-trained employees being stolen by other companies now ask, "If other organizations don't want him or her, why should I?"

Gelatt (1998) supported that position with his self–system synergy model, which stated that organizations will be more successful if they support their employees' self-reliance, interdependence, and continuous learning. The positive outcome that results from individuals and the "system" both paying attention to each other's needs is what he called synergy. Dawis, England, and Lofquist (1964) anticipated the current focus on worker/organization interdependence with their work adjustment theory, which stated, in its simplest terms, that workers must be both satisfied and satisfactory.

The needs of modern companies for a flexible workforce are clear. Career self-reliance and resiliency was the theme of a 1996 symposium on the new workforce (Career Action Center, 1996). Speakers from a variety of large companies, including Chrysler, Shell, and Intel, addressed these issues. Workforce resiliency was defined as an individual responsibility and a shared commitment (Career Action Center, 1996). Some of the personal attributes identified included:

- focused but flexible
- dedicated to continuous learning
- committed to personal excellence

Some of the organizational attributes identified were:

- offer opportunity to do challenging work
- foster honest and open communication
- build an environment that integrates these values into the business strategy

This emphasis on resiliency by business and industry makes it even clearer why we have an obligation to help students become more resilient.

There is also a growing body of research that identifies resiliency with other positive emotional states. Novick (1998) stated that resiliency and emotional intelligence were related, and that key elements of both were self-esteem and self-efficacy. She wrote that resiliency required "the ability to see the difficulty as a problem that can be worked on, overcome, changed, endured, or resolved in some way, …an ability to know when 'enough is enough' and a capacity to develop a range of flexible strategies and skills to bring to bear on the problem" (p. 201). Noonan (1999) correlated brief intervention strategies with protective factors that have been identified with resiliency, including support, high expectations, and life skills training.

It seems clear that resiliency is a "good thing," that it is necessary for success in the world of work in the third millennium, and that it helps individuals lead more satisfying lives. The question then becomes how do we foster career resilience? Gelatt (1991) influentially proposed a method of fostering career resiliency with his series of paradoxes related to career decisions: (1) be focused and flexible about what you want, (2) be aware and wary about what you know, (3) be objective and optimistic about what you believe, and (4) be practical and magical about what you do (pp. 7–10). His approach is one of "using *both* [emphasis added] rational and intuitive techniques" (cover) to make decisions. In preparing students to both decide and be prepared to change, we help them develop resiliency. When we imply that a career decision is a one-time event, we do a disservice. The first bump in the road, to employ a pathway metaphor, leaves students surprised and unsure of what to do next. It may also leave them feeling betrayed and make it harder to "pop back up." Indeed, one of the themes we encounter in my adult career counseling center is just that. Our clients say things like, "I did all the right things. I worked hard and played by the rules. It just isn't fair that I have to regroup. This time I want to make a decision with a guarantee."

Addressing the need to go beyond merely demonstrating the need for resiliency, Mitchell, Levin, and Krumbotz's (1999) work on planned happenstance teaches students how to become more resilient by capitalizing on opportunities. They identified five skills necessary to take advantage of planned happenstance:

1. Curiosity: exploring new learning opportunities
2. Persistence: exerting effort despite setbacks
3. Flexibility: changing attitudes and circumstances
4. Optimism: viewing new opportunities as possible and attainable
5. Risk Taking: taking actions in the face of uncertain outcomes

These five skills would be considered by most to be hallmarks of resilience. Mitchell et al.'s cognitively based approach includes restructuring familiar career development activities, such as the information interview, and encompasses a four-step process that can be taught. These four steps can be summarized as (1) normalize planned happenstance, (2) use curiosity to develop opportunities, (3) create chance events, and (4) overcome blocks to action. In the information interview, as an example, the client would be encouraged not only to ask the typical questions about what the person does and what they like and dislike about their work, but also to talk to others in the waiting room, to look around them for other jobs that might be of interest to them, and to be alert to chance events that might lead to other opportunities. I once obtained a summer job in New York City, after an extremely frustrating day of job seeking, by taking advantage of planned happenstance. When I arrived at a local "Y" to see if they had any openings, they said they did not have time to interview me as they had a big mailing to get out. I offered to stay and help, and stayed for the rest of the summer!

Let us look at some commonly used career development paradigms from this perspective. In Michigan, as in many states, there is a system of six career pathways that is used to organize job families (Michigan Department of Career Development, 2002). They are arts and communication; business, management, marketing, and technology; engineering, manufacturing, and industrial technology; health sciences; human services; and natural resources and agriculture. As in Michigan, most systems are developed along the same lines as John Holland's classification system (1959), with jobs organized around themes similar to his Realistic, Investigative, Artistic, Social, Enterprising, and Conventional categories. Many interest inventories and computer-assisted career guidance systems use similar taxonomies around which to organize job families or actual job titles. These systems differ in their categories but are similar in their intention, which is to create a classification scheme for students that allows them to narrow down their focus. Although school counselors may recommend exploring all pathways, the usual procedure is for students to choose one, as early as middle school, and make course selections based on that pathway. It is often also recommended that students explore volunteer work or part-time jobs in the same pathway. While it is wonderful to encourage such exploration and attention to career development, a more resiliency-fostering process might be to expect every student to explore all pathways and develop a series of plans — or alternate routes, if you wish to follow the pathway metaphor.

There are many ways to do this. It can be done through classroom guidance activities, through expanding service-learning requirements, through assignments in core classes, and through special activities such as senior projects. For example, a classroom guidance activity that promotes exploring many arenas is Shazam: You Are a Human Cat! (Lloyd, 1997; Sullivan, 2003). In this activity students are asked to imagine that they have nine lives to devote to different career paths. After they list nine options, they can look to see if there are common themes, if they could be done sequentially, if one might help prepare the student for another, etc. The point being made is not only to look at dreams, but to envision that a variety of occupations may lay in their future. There are many resources for career activities that can be used to develop resiliency, for example, Pope and Minor (2000).

Career day speakers can be invited to discuss the route they have taken to get to their present position, as well as describing the work they do, as is traditional. Career day organizers should ensure that many of the invited speakers have followed circuitous routes and should encourage them to describe failures and false starts as well as successes and direct pathways.

Service learning requirements exist in many high schools. The selection of learning activity is often left up to the student, but it can be structured so as to provide a mini-experience in a chosen career path. To develop a broader base, as I am proposing, students could be required to engage in several briefer service-learning experiences, associated with different career pathways or Holland (1959) categories.

It is often recommended that career exploration be a part of core curricular experiences. One way for this to happen is for teachers to include career content in their normal classroom work. Keyboard classes, for example, can have students developing resumes and cover letters; speech classes can have students practicing job interviews. Resilience building can be fostered by having students in English, for example, read biographies or autobiographies of people who have failed and bounced back. They can be asked to write essays about these people, and about their own failures and how they have recovered, or what they wish they had been able to do. Science teachers can help students understand that most scientific progress includes false starts, repeated failure, and the necessity of rethinking established beliefs. All of these lessons are learning opportunities to understand and foster resilience.

Senior projects have been touted as a way to make sense out of the last semester of high school, which for many students is a time to play. Once college acceptances are in, once graduation is determined, many fortunate students have little to do except pass their classes, and they often need very few credits to graduate. Senior projects can be as minimal as an extended job shadowing, or as extensive as a semester working half-time in a chosen career area, with writing assignments and other academic requirements. This kind of opportunity to explore the "real world" of work can be invaluable. It can foster resiliency if students are asked to explore at least two areas and if they are asked to gather information, as suggested earlier when describing career day content, about the paths taken by those whom they are shadowing.

The American School Counselor Association (ASCA) has developed a model program, part of which describes career development — along with academic and personal social development (2003). Although the word resiliency is not used in the standards, it is implied in such indicators as, "Apply decision-making skills to career planning, course selection, and *career transition* [emphasis added]" (p. 83) and "Understand that the changing workplace requires lifelong learning and acquiring new skills" (p. 84). School counselors are often pressured by parents and administrators to have their students decide. The idea is that this saves wasted time and money. But, as we have indicated earlier, deciding must be accompanied by an understanding of how to change if it is to lead to long-term career resiliency.

Janas (2002) suggests 20 techniques to foster resiliency in children. They include practicing unconditional positive acceptance, communicating realistic standards, providing opportunities to defer gratification, emphasizing opportunities to be part of something greater than self, sharing your humor, and modeling being a resilient adult. Herr (1992) advised counselors to focus on empowerment as a way of encouraging personal flexibility, a similar concept to resiliency. He concluded, "New paradigms of career counseling are required that will emphasize personal empowerment and competence within the complexities of changing educational, psychological, cross-cultural and cross-national contexts" (p. 15).

How might traditional career development programs be modified? Several books from the self-help genre give us some clues. In the best-seller *Who Moved My Cheese?* (1998), Johnson presents an allegory of mice that resist change to the point of starvation, and compares them to mice that accept change and move on. The lessons learned by the resilient mice are:

- change happens
- anticipate change
- monitor change
- adapt to change quickly
- change
- enjoy change
- be ready to quickly change again and again

The underlying message is that not only is change constant, but also one must embrace change and see it as leading to more positive outcomes. I am not sure every dislocated worker would agree with the belief that all outcomes are positive, but none can disagree with the reality that change is constant.

In *Going to Plan B,* Schlossberg and Robinson (1996) discussed the resiliency that is required when anticipated things do not happen, *non-events* in their terminology. They posited a series of responses — acknowledging, easing, refocusing, reshaping — that is necessary to cope with these non-events. We would call that resiliency. They also suggested that there is a way to determine the impact of the non-events. Is the individual involved seen as hopeful or hopeless? Is the transition sudden or gradual? Is it seen as in or out of the person's control? And is it seen as positive, negative, or neutral? Elsewhere Schlossberg suggested that these parameters apply to transitions generally, not just non-events (Schlossberg, Waters, & Goodman, 1995). Her 4 S model provides a system for assessing individuals' ability to cope with or manage a particular transition. By looking at the situation, the individual (or self), the support, and the person's knowledge of appropriate coping strategies, a counselor can determine where assistance is needed. One could call this a formula for helping engender resiliency. Strategies were identified as actions that changed the situation, changed the meaning of the situation, or if neither of these were possible, managed the attendant stress.

One implication of the idea of changing the meaning of the transition is that to foster career resiliency we need to instill hope. Seligman (1998) addressed this issue in his book *Learned Optimism.* After much research, he concluded that "the remarkable attribute of resilience in the face of defeat need not remain a mystery. It was not an inborn trait; it could be acquired" (p. 30). It becomes clear then that to foster career resiliency, and life resiliency in general, we need to *teach* optimism.

How can we do that? Seligman proposes teaching skills that transform pessimists into optimists. They are:

1. *Distraction.* This is a process of shifting focus away from distressing thoughts and toward more positive ones. The admonition, "Don't think about it!" doesn't seem to work. The admonition, "Think about something positive instead," actually does seem to work. In teaching resiliency, we might, for example, use reframing statements to help students learn to be more optimistic. We can help students change, "Math is too hard for me; I can't learn it," to, "I know how to get the help I need to learn the aspects of algebra that are puzzling to me." We can help them change, "Work is simply drudgery. No one in my family likes their work. I don't expect to either," to, "I would like to be the first in my family to have a satisfying career. What can I do to increase the likelihood of that happening?"

2. *Disputation.* This is a process of actually arguing with a thought—either internal self-talk or negative statements that have been made by others. Three of Seligman's suggestions for disputation are discussed below:

   a. *Evidence.* Ask yourself, what is the actual evidence that this thought or accusation is true? Find contrary evidence. For example, if you are thinking that because you did poorly on a test, that you are a terrible student, remind yourself of all of the tests you have done well on, or remind yourself that you perform better in practical situations.

b. *Alternatives.* Ask yourself, what are the alternative explanations for this event besides thinking I am a poor student? Was the test on material you had not studied? Were you unduly anxious? Was the test format one that is harder for you than others?

c. *Implications.* Consider your catastrophic expectations and then examine whether they are really likely. In the above example, your catastrophic expectation might be that you will never get into any college, that your dreams of becoming a veterinarian are over, or that you will lose your sports eligibility. Is it really likely that one test score will do all that? (p. 217–220)

Seligman's techniques can be taught to students as part of a comprehensive guidance program to enhance career resiliency. Coupled with experiences to increase knowledge of opportunities, a reduced focus on a decision, and an increased focus on the decision-making process, optimism can be a powerful attribute.

I have attempted in this chapter to identify a number of other techniques for fostering career resiliency. Developing career resiliency is not only important, it is possible. It is necessary to combine information about the world of work and its requirements for flexibility, adaptability, and resiliency with techniques to foster generally resilient students.

Chapter 5

Linking Resiliency With the School
Counseling Program

The role of the school counselor has evolved over the last two decades, paralleling changes in society and in public expectations about the school's role in raising young children to be productive citizens. Changes in counseling practice fall generally into three categories: involvement with classroom or group teaching; use of evidence-based programs, curricula, or strategies; and involvement in schoolwide environmental change.

The traditional role of the school counselor was focused on scheduling, career planning, and mental health crises. As counselors have become more aware of students' changing needs at various developmental stages, they have moved toward a model of providing developmentally appropriate guidance lessons in classrooms in addition to traditional one-on-one and schoolwide services. As a result, there is less emphasis on providing individual mental health counseling or on the clerical and management roles of scheduling or discipline. In their new role, counselors are now teaching and modeling life, decision-making, problem-solving, and conflict resolution skills. They are working with teachers to improve classroom management and conflict resolution in order to facilitate the academic mission of the school.

Traditionally, principals, counselors, and teachers have used professional wisdom and principles of best practice to guide their activities. However, research over the past 15 to 20 years now provides guidance for reforming educational practice to enhance students' academic success. Such research allows educators to compare the effectiveness of various practices and can guide the implementation of programs, strategies, and processes that are most likely to meet the school's goals for student development. The current challenge for educators is to implement these evidence-based practices widely.

Another change affecting counselors is a shift in focus away from changing individuals and toward changing environments. Traditional research in social behavioral sciences and education took a deficit approach to studying human behavior and development. Groups of students with an identified deficit—from doing poorly in school to delinquency, alcohol and other drug use, or pregnancy—were studied extensively, and interventions specific to their needs were developed. Following a pullout model, these students were separated for intervention within the school setting.

In contrast to the traditional approach, an emerging body of research examines those students who become happy, confident, competent, and caring adults despite growing up in disadvantaged or high-stress environments (Werner & Smith, 1992). From this research, characteristics of both the children and their environment that account for their overcoming the odds and having successful developmental outcomes can be identified. Many educators, including counselors, have become interested in this research and are seeking ways to modify the local school environment to promote resiliency among all students.

Providing a Continuum of Services

In Chapters 2, 3, and 4, we discussed the important roles that school counselors can play in helping students avoid risk-taking behaviors, removing barriers to students' academic achievement, and assisting students to understand the importance of resiliency in their career planning and development. To carry out this role, school counselors must provide a continuum of services.

In a continuum of services, barriers to learning are addressed through a comprehensive, multifaceted, and integrated spectrum of intervention services. Because many of the problems that youth face today are complicated and multidimensional, multiple levels of intervention must be available and coordinated so that students can receive timely assistance appropriate to their level of need. Three levels of intervention are commonly identified in the literature: universal, selected, and indicated.

Universal
Universal intervention consists of strategies, such as assertiveness training or decision-making skills, that are presented to all students to protect against risk-taking behavior and promote positive development. If all students are taught basic life skills through universal intervention, and the environment supports and reinforces

these skills, the number of students who need more intensive levels of intervention can be reduced.

Selected

Some students who are at high risk of negative outcomes because of chronic situations or temporary problems need additional instruction or support to prevent their progression to negative behaviors. Recently Blum and colleagues (2002) have shown that students who are alienated from school are at high risk for engaging in risky health behaviors. A selected intervention based on this finding would identify those students with low measures of bonding to school and work to increase their ties to their school in the hope of heading off negative health outcomes down the road.

Indicated

Finally, a small percentage of any population will exhibit problem behavior; it is this segment of students that is served by indicated programs. Services need to be available, for example, to prevent the progression from experimentation with cigarettes to habitual use. Thus, a student who has been caught with cigarettes on a field trip might be a candidate for a more intensive, or indicated, smoking intervention than the generic health information on the dangers of tobacco that the entire student body receives in health class. The indicated category would also include aftercare programs provided for students who return to school following inpatient drug or alcohol treatment. These students need extra support to ensure that they successfully reintegrate into the school and do not relapse.

School Counseling Program Models

Historically, there has been little practitioner-oriented research that could guide school counseling practice. In the past decade, however, research that directly impacts counseling practice has mushroomed. During the same period, the role of schools, and concurrently the role of school counselors, has changed to meet the increasingly complex demands on the public education system resulting from a technology- and information-based society.

The current approach to school counseling originated in the late 1960s and early 1970s, led by the work of such leaders in the field as Norman Gysbers and Robert Myrick. They developed organizational models designed to move the school counseling program away from its previous role of scheduling and crisis intervention to providing more comprehensive services within the schools.

The Comprehensive Guidance Program Model

The Comprehensive Guidance Program Model (CGPM) was first published in 1974. It has been revised and expanded since that time at both the university and local school district levels. Today nearly half of the states in the United States have adopted this model. The ultimate outcome of a CGPM is "life career" development (Gysbers & Henderson, 1997). Life career development is defined as "self-development over a person's life span through integration of roles, settings, and events in the person's life" (p. 9). In this definition, career does not mean only one's occupation but includes the roles an individual assumes as worker, consumer, citizen, parent, etc., in various settings such as home, work, school, or community. Thus the term *life career development* in the context of CGPM encompasses the total individual.

This approach also focuses on issues of human development. Myrick (1987) points out the developmental approach "considers the nature of human development" (p. 32), and "involves an interaction between what the person is given genetically and the different environments in which the person lives and grows" (p. 33). This paradigm, therefore, focuses on a systematic, planned counseling program that fosters social, emotional, physical, moral, and cognitive growth by providing direct intervention and support services to enhance the efforts of parents, teachers, and other school personnel.

Ivey and Goncalves (1988) have suggested that counseling, in general, has a primary goal of facilitating development. They believe that a developmental approach dictates that the counseling process start with the client rather than a theoretical approach or the needs of the institution. Developmental approaches are particularly effective for prevention because certain types of problems can be prevented through developmentally appropriate interventions. From research, J. V. Peterson and Nisenholz (1999) have identified five multidimensional and interactive principles of human development:

1. Growth is a continuous, lifelong process.
2. Growth is sequential and unique.
3. Growth is the unfolding of the programmed genetic code (deoxyribonucleic acid or DNA).
4. Growth is integrative, in that all of the human systems work together and the cognitive, physical, emotional, and spiritual dimensions become integrated.
5. Growth occurs in stages.

To meet these developmental needs, as well as a school's need for mental health services, the CGPM proposed by Gysbers and Moore

(1974) and elaborated at both the university and practice levels contains four program components: guidance curriculum, individual planning, responsive services, and systems support.

Guidance Curriculum. A guidance curriculum (a universal intervention) can be delivered either in structured groups of any size or in a classroom setting. Within the classroom, counselors and teachers may team teach activities or units that support the competencies of self-knowledge and interpersonal skills, life role settings and events, and life career planning. Because of the increasing emphasis on academic standards and achievement, lessons in the guidance curriculum are often designed to promote academic skills as well as socioemotional ones. Counselors can use literature or other academic content to teach these competencies in ways that promote the academic skills students will need to be successful in life.

Group activities in a guidance curriculum may take many different forms. For example, a counselor may discuss the middle school class schedule with all the fifth graders in an assembly. Later, the counselor could meet with individual classes to answer any questions and to help students complete scheduling forms. Another large-group activity might be a career day or college day. Counselors might gather all students who are interested in financial aid for college, or all students interested in pursuing a military career, for special meetings based on their particular interests. The guidance curriculum serves to reach a large number of students, providing information and skills in a developmental sequence. Use of evidence-based programs, curricula, or strategies greatly enhances the effectiveness of the guidance curriculum.

Individual Planning. Whereas the guidance curriculum and large-group educational activities might provide sufficient support for some students, others may need individual help with planning. In this capacity, the counselor becomes an expert in appraisal, advisement, and placement. This individual planning consists of activities that help students move forward with their own personal and career development. Examples are filling out a schedule for high school or selecting an appropriate postsecondary educational institution. Ideally, this process should occur in close collaboration with parents and other significant adults in the young person's life.

Responsive Services. Problems and crises are an inevitable feature of life. Some students and their families may need the intervention of a counselor at key points in time. Counselors provide responsive services in a number of ways. Often they advise parents, teachers, or administrators on ways to deal with student behavior or academic problems. For students who are having particular problems or issues with relationships, personal concerns, or normal developmental tasks, short-term personal counseling may be provided either in small groups or individually. In a CGPM, counselors generally do not provide intense psychotherapy or long-term counseling services with either individual students or their families.

Once a need has been identified, counselors in a CGPM serve as experts in the referral of students to appropriate mental health agencies, employment and training programs, vocational rehabilitation programs, juvenile justice programs, or social services. Effective counselors are knowledgeable of all the various service providers within the community and are able to facilitate the referral process.

Systems Support. This last component of the four includes a variety of activities that counselors engage in to provide support for the school environment so that the school runs more smoothly. In some school settings, systems support is a catchall category encompassing myriad unrelated activities such as lunch duty, bus duty, or playground duty. Within the Comprehensive Guidance Program Model, such duties are not considered appropriate support services because they underutilize the specialized skills and training of the professional counselor. More appropriate examples of support services include sitting on committees or advisory boards engaged in outreach to the community and to families. They also often provide professional development for faculty, particularly in the area of human development. Counselors are often responsible for monitoring evaluation and development as well as staff and community public relations.

The CGPM not only identifies program components, but it also indicates the suggested amount of time that the counselor ought to be spending in various activities (see Table 5.1).

As Table 5.1 shows, these percentages are distributed differently depending on the age level and developmental needs of the students. For example, classroom interaction occupies a significant percentage of the elementary school counselor's time, whereas a high school counselor would spend less time in the classroom and more on individual planning.

The CGPM has served to define the role and mission of school counselors nationally for several decades. Recently, however, changes in the educational landscape, such as standards-based reform, high-stakes testing, school safety issues, the continuing achievement gap,

Table 5.1. Suggested Distribution of Total Counselor Time

CGPM COMPONENTS	COUNSELOR'S TIME		
	Elementary School	Middle/Junior School	High School
Guidance Curriculum	35–45%	25–35%	15–25%
Individual Planning	5–10	15–25	25–35
Responsive Services	30–40	30–40	25–35
Systems Support	10–15	10–15	15–20

Source: Reprinted with permission from Gysbers, N.,& Henderson,P., (1974).*Comprehensive guidance programs that work—II.* Greensboro, NC: ERIC/ CASS.

and budget cuts, have led to re-examination of current school counseling practice and models. Two groups have proposed alternative models based on CGPM to guide school counselors in this age of accountability and reform. The American School Counselor Association (ASCA) has recently published a model for school counseling programs (Bowers & Hatch, 2002; American School Counselor Association, 2003). The second model comes from the Washington, D.C., based nonprofit Education Trust. Supported by funds from the DeWitt Wallace–Reader's Digest Fund and MetLife, the Education Trust in 1996 began a multiyear initiative to transform school counseling. Their work resulted in identifying skills counselors need to meet the changing roles in schools. (Martin, 2002). The following discussion describes each of these initiatives.

The ASCA National Model: A Framework for School Counseling Programs

The next generation of the comprehensive guidance program has been developed by ASCA, a worldwide nonprofit professional organization for school counselors. Providing professional development, publications and other resources, research, and advocacy to nearly 14,000 professional school counselors around the globe, ASCA is respected as the leading professional association for school counselors.

The advantage of the ASCA-sponsored national model is that it unifies individual school counselors in the practice of their discipline. As one counselor said, "The National Model for School Counseling Programs will help school counselors become one vision and one voice for students' academic success" (Bowers & Hatch, 2002, p. 15). The ASCA National Model for School Counseling Programs has as a goal to connect school counseling with current school reform movements that emphasize academic achievement. The model focuses school counseling efforts in three domains: academic, career, and personal/ social. In support of those three areas, the model has several features. It is comprehensive in its design, emphasizing the three areas of the continuum of services: universal, selected, and indicated. The model is preventive, emphasizing a proactive approach to addressing the three areas. It identifies developmentally appropriate activities delivered systematically at all grade levels in each domain area. Activities related to the model are conducted collaboratively with all members of the school community, including families and stakeholders in the community.

Under this model, a counselor's role within a school is balanced across activities in four domains: foundation, delivery system, management system, and accountability system. The foundation is the philosophy, mission, and ASCA national standards and competencies. The delivery system consists of the guidance curriculum, individual planning with students, responsive services, and support systems. The management system is critical in helping the counselor manage time. Within this area are activities related to planning, analyzing data, monitoring student progress, and making agreements with the school leadership. The accountability system calls for counselors to report on the results of their activities, not just their completion. It is suggested that counselors have an advisory board to provide oversight and guidance.

Within the model are four themes that support the four areas of activities in the model. They also support the development and maintenance of environments that support resiliency. These are leadership, advocacy, collaboration and teaming, and systemic change.

Leadership. By collaborating with other professionals in the school and the community, counselors can help to implement schoolwide changes and reforms that will benefit all students. The model encourages school counselors to become catalysts for change to facilitate academic and social growth in all students. A component of leadership is having reliable and valid information about new evidence-based strategies, programs, or curricula that will support the school's mission.

Advocacy. Counselors have traditionally been advocates for the educational and socioemotional needs of individual students. They can actively work with students to remove barriers to learning and help identify systemic barriers that threaten to thwart the academic success of certain groups of students.

Collaboration and Teaming. Most activities in today's schools are complex and require team planning, coordination, monitoring, and evaluation. Given their interpersonal and organizational background and training, school counselors are ideally situated to develop and coordinate planning teams.

Systemic Change. Systemic change involves an organized, coordinated effort to make lasting change in a school. It involves rethinking the way things are done and identifying more effective or efficient structures or activities to meet new needs for student achievement.

National School Counselor Training Initiative (NSCTI)

For the past several years the National School Counselor Training Initiative (NSCTI) of the Education Trust has explored the role of school counseling in this era of school reform. The initiative's goal is to make school counseling central to the evolving mission of schools by building on traditional counselor skills that can make a unique contribution to school reform. A central component of this approach is the use of data to direct interventions aimed at removing the barriers to learning.

In the NSCTI model, the school counselor has two goals:

- Achieve equity and social justice for students
- Increase student learning and achievement

In this model, school counselors remove the barriers to learning through addressing five skill areas: leadership, teamwork and collaboration, use of data, counseling, and advocacy.

Leadership. Leadership is not defined by a role such as principal or superintendent. Leadership is a characteristic that can be best seen in the way a person handles change. A leader takes a proactive stance in any organization, continually asking, "How can we make this better?" to foster a culture of constant improvement. Leaders have visions and beliefs that they are not reluctant to share with others.

Teamwork and Collaboration. By necessity, leadership is shared within a school. Teams are involved in assessing students with behavioral or academic issues, academic subjects are often team taught, and parents and other community members are involved in numerous school issues ranging from budget to curriculum. Using their skills in group facilitation and knowledge of development, counselors can play a leadership role in teams and collaborative activities, as well as in teaching and modeling appropriate behavior and skills (e.g., conflict resolution, decision making, and problem solving) in those situations.

Use of Data. Using data for decision making is central in the NSCTI model. Data can help the counselor identify both successes and situations that need attention. Using data to identify where resources can best be utilized is essential given current tight budgets and the focus on accountability. For example, River Bend Elementary School experienced a significant drop in third-grade reading scores. The district curriculum specialist recommended that the reading program at River Bend be changed. The counselor, however, looked at the characteristics of the students who were in the lowest quartile, noticing that these children had lower attendance rates than their peers who scored better. Given this information, the staff at River Bend decided that the best course of action was to work on the truancy issue, rather than replace the reading program.

Counseling. In any school, responsive counseling services are needed. Working with individual children, groups of children, or family members remains an essential part of the school counselor's position.

Advocacy. Although most counselors have informally taken on the role of advocates for children, there is a new urgency to become more active in this area. School counselors are in an ideal position to work for social justice and advocate for all students. Because the disparity in academic achievement between White and non-White students continues, counselors must work to promote educational and academic excellence for all students within the school. In interviews with parents of freshmen at a Big Ten university, parents who had never attended college reported that the school counselor was instrumental in helping their children down the path that would lead to attendance at a major university. A major part of advocacy is to develop a data-driven advocacy plan. Such a plan provides a road map for systemic change that will make the system more responsive to the educational and developmental needs of all children.

Evidence-Based Program Strategies

Fortunately, several decades of research and evaluation studies have identified strategies, programs, and curricula that have shown efficacy in changing mental health outcomes (including substance abuse and violence) and increasing student achievement. If they use evidence-based programs, counselors can be assured that their guidance curriculum has a higher likelihood of meeting their goals for student healthy behavior and normal growth.

A program, curriculum, or strategy can fit into any one of the following categories:

1. *Professional wisdom.* Up until the last ten years, professional wisdom was a benchmark for identifying topics, curricula, and strategies within the guidance curriculum. If the curriculum flowed well and the students were engaged, then it was judged appropriate. Yet the value of lessons based solely on professional wisdom is questionable, because they lack a coherent theoretical rationale or research-based evidence of efficacy.

2. *Best practice.* Best practice is a consensus of professional wisdom, usually based on the agreement of a number of expert practitioners, regarding the best way to address a particular subject. Sometimes best practice is driven by marketing of a particular product. For example, a particular curriculum or textbook may be so well marketed that many people in the field use it and support each other in its use. Because a critical mass of professionals is using the curriculum or practice, it gains credibility regardless of whether or not it meets the intended goal. In fact, some popular programs or curricula actually have been shown to be ineffective.

3. *Theory-driven.* The next level of program or curriculum is that based on a theoretical approach. The logic model is that if educators follow the theory, a positive outcome is expected. Examples of such an approach are the development of lessons or approaches based on Gardner's theory of multiple intelligences (Gardner, 1993) or Goleman's theory of emotional intelligence (Goleman, 1995). These theories have merit because of their sound application of the principles of human development. Yet, programs following theories such as these may not be shown through rigorous evaluation studies to produce better outcomes.

   As another example, suppose researchers find that the more active a student is, the higher his or her math scores on standardized tests tend to be. One could take that finding and develop a theory-based program that would increase the amount of physical education for children with low math scores. Although this approach is based on research, there is no guarantee that the intervention would achieve the intended result.

4. *Evidence-based.* The highest standard of effectiveness for a program or curriculum is research evidence. This evidence is gathered through rigorous evaluation studies designed with random selection, large enough numbers of participants to detect differences, and a comparison group that is measured at the same time as the experimental group but receives no intervention. Thus, one can compare the outcomes of students who receive the intervention with those of similar students at the same period of time who receive no intervention. Intervention is shown to be effective if over time the students who receive that intervention in fact do better on the outcome of interest than those students who receive no intervention.

5. *Model programs.* In the past decade, expert panels and reviewers have identified programs and strategies designed to teach social skills and prevent drug use and violence. Counselors can find listings of evidence-based programs on the Center for Substance Abuse Prevention (prevention.samhsa.gov) and the U.S. Department of Education (www.ed.gov) Web sites.

Thus, in terms of accountability, using evidence-based or theory-driven programs, curricula, or strategies demonstrates a level of accountability that ensures that time and resources are spent on interventions that have known efficacy. Although it is still important to monitor student outcomes, the community can be assured the students are receiving the highest-quality materials.

Promoting Student Resiliency Within the School Counseling Program: Two Case Studies

Case Study 1: Easing Transition to High School

Tina Roberts was a traditional counselor in a high school in a large district. One of her responsibilities was to orient the eighth-grade students to course scheduling and other issues involved in the transition to high school. Traditionally, Tina had held a large assembly at each of the three middle schools, where she presented all the eighth graders with the necessary information. She also was available on three or four additional days at each site to answer any student or parent questions that might arise. This activity consumed most of her time in the months of April and May.

When the school board mandated that juniors complete a certain number of hours of community service, Tina offered willing juniors the opportunity to participate in this transition activity. She worked for a semester, one period a day, with a class of 30 juniors. They were trained in all the issues involved in the transition to high school. They created PowerPoint presentations to ensure consistent presentation of information across schools. They role-played interactions with parents and students to ensure they were prepared to answer questions and help the students feel confident about the transition to high school.

During the scheduling months, pairs of trained students from the class visited each eighth-grade classroom in each of the three feeder schools. They gave the standard presentation and then personally answered questions. Tina was available to field any questions or concerns outside of the presentation, but received virtually no phone calls or requests for follow-up information or troubleshooting.

Using these students as a resource freed Tina to attend to other counseling duties during the months of April and May. In addition, both the juniors and the eighth graders benefited. The juniors had a rich learning experience that included presentation skills, computer skills, and counseling skills. The eighth graders had more personal attention to their concerns about the transition to high school. In addition, they had an identified upper classman who could serve as both a role model and a source of assistance if needed.

The eighth-grade teachers and counselors were pleased with the new system, because student questions were answered at the initial orientation, and students rarely needed to take additional time outside of their academic classes to resolve issues. Thus this activity enhanced the resiliency of all the participating students and gave both eighth-grade teachers and Tina additional time for other academic activities.

Case Study 2: Teaching Conflict Resolution and Violence Prevention

In another situation, Sean Kosinski, an elementary school counselor, was asked by his principal to teach conflict resolution and violence prevention. After a year of going to each classroom on a weekly basis to present lessons on these topics, Sean reviewed discipline referrals and realized that the number of fights and conflicts had not decreased significantly. Sean went to the Internet and looked at state and federal government Web sites that identified theory-based and evidence-based approaches to conflict resolution and violence prevention. He identified two approaches that seemed to have the most credibility. One was various models of peer mediation to resolve disputes or altercations between students, and the other was a cluster of several evidence-based violence prevention curricula.

Through the Internet, he was able to preview a number of these curricula and communicate with educators in other schools and districts who had used either violence prevention curricula or peer mediation programs. He identified three that would mesh with the characteristics of his elementary school and ordered review copies. Once those arrived, he asked the principal to call a meeting of teachers representing all grades so he could present and explain the options. Teachers, who were likewise frustrated with the continuing conflicts among the students, were enthusiastic about Sean's approach. He became certified as a trainer in an evidence-based violence prevention curriculum and brought in trainers from the local mental health agency to help facilitate a peer mediation program.

The next spring, Sean trained a representative teacher at each grade level in the violence prevention program, so that the next fall he could begin co-teaching the curriculum with the grade-level teachers. By the end of the fall semester, the teachers were sufficiently comfortable with the curriculum that Sean only taught certain lessons at certain grades. He used the time that he would have spent in the classroom to establish the peer mediation program by identifying and training peer mediators and organizing a mediation protocol.

In both cases, Tina and Sean provided the schools with the support of a trained counselor. However, they shifted their time allocation so that they also trained and empowered other people to function in a resiliency– and mental health–promoting role. They both accomplished systemic change within their schools. Each one still provided some type of guidance curriculum. Individual planning for students will continue to be part of their responsibilities as will responsive services. However, much of their time now is spent in creating and supporting a system that promotes resiliency in all students and teachers. Teachers and students have increased their capacity to manage situations and to bring about change independently.

Program Models and Resiliency: Summary

A resiliency approach is complementary to models of counseling that focus on changing the environment to be more supportive of achievement and success for all students. School counselors can influence more children by helping to create and maintain positive school environments based on the resiliency principles of care and concern, meaningful participation, and high expectations than they can by sitting in an office counseling individual students.

Chapter 6

Counselor and Educator Practices That Promote Student Resiliency

When Anton was five, he was diagnosed with attention deficit hyperactivity disorder (ADHD). He struggled in school and ended up dropping out after the 10th grade. Ten years later he is a sous chef in a busy downtown bistro. Today, he sees his ADHD as a benefit in his job. People with regular attention spans would not be successful in a hectic kitchen with hundreds of different tasks that have to come together in a meal that will please the customer's palate.

A strength-based view of the world is central to resiliency. Resilient children like Anton are able to overcome the adversities or stresses in their lives because they are able to focus on their strengths and develop talents that let them outperform expectations. This fact translates into a mandate for counselors and educators to design and implement programs, systems, and practices that follow a strength-based approach. Much of a counselor's typical training focuses on diagnostic means for determining a child's present functioning and future prognosis in academic and social arenas. This perspective inherently focuses on deficits, that is, determining what is wrong with the child or what needs to be fixed. A strength-based, resiliency-supporting approach turns this perspective around, in that practitioners have "a greater concern for [children's] strengths and competencies and [efforts] to discover mutually how these personal resources can be applied to building solutions" (Clark, 1998, p. 46).

Strength-based practices have been shown to be effective in multiple settings and with a variety of types of children, ranging from infants and toddlers with disabilities (Campbell, Milbourne, & Silverman, 2001) to juvenile offenders (Clark, 1998) to an entire department within a school district (K. Frey, personal communication, 2000). Strength-based approaches are not complex, but they do require a shift in mindset, from focusing on the problem to focusing on the solution, and from focusing on causes to focusing on results.

A deficit-based problem-solving approach starts with identifying what the problem is, what is not working, or what is wrong. A search for a cause or someone or something to blame follows, leading to the development of plans to prevent the problem from recurring. This approach has several limitations. First, the search for blame tends to make people defensive and resistant to change. Second, once a cause is identified, people tend to focus in that direction, which limits the breadth and creativity of their problem solving (Oakley & Krug, 1991). In contrast, a strength-based approach begins by examining what is working. From there, the focus moves to identifying desired steps to build on the strengths even further in the future. As a result, no one is placed on the defensive, which encourages participants in the planning process to put forward more, and more innovative, ideas. The focus is on making the future better, not on correcting the mistakes of the past.

Resiliency is developed through regular daily experiences and interactions that foster students' social and academic success. A structured program or specific curriculum does not accomplish this; a positive, protective environment does. In creating and maintaining a school climate that supports resiliency, the importance of day-to-day interactions between school personnel and students cannot be overstated. Children pay much more attention to deeds than to words. What counselors and teachers do when they interact with children is a lot more powerful than anything they say to students or any words printed on the mission statement that hangs in the office. Caring adults look past the outside of a child and see promise (Werner, 1999). By taking the lead in modeling caring behavior, counselors can encourage other school personnel to do the same.

Accepting children however they come is essential. As one counselor said, "Families are sending us the best kids they have." Students do not have control over their individual strengths and weaknesses, their family income or circumstances, their ethnic background, or any of the other myriad of dimensions on which educators analyze them. Labeling students and their families can be very destructive. Children who hear such labels may internalize them as indicating that something is wrong with them or the people they love. What do children and their families feel when they hear a label? Rejection and exclusion. In contrast, a strength-based approach guides counselors and educators in keeping the focus on the child—and whatever is good about that child—rather than on external factors.

Strength-Based Counselor and Educator Practices

Following are some simple ways to demonstrate caring, concern, and interest in a child. By modeling these behaviors in their own interactions, counselors can encourage other educators in the school to do the same. It is easy to underestimate the positive effect of such small gestures as learning children's names; smiling at them; talking to them at their eye level; asking about their day (and listening to the answer); attending and showing support for their outside activities; and using short, informal interactions to seek their hidden talents and unique interests. These simple actions convey to a student that the counselor values him or her as an individual.

Another opportunity for counselors to promote resiliency-reinforcing behaviors among school staff occurs during discussions or conferences about children. When discussing a child with a teacher, administrator, or other school staff, the school counselor should model a strength-based approach by always starting the conversation with identifying the child's strengths. If others tend to fixate on the child's problems, the counselor should steer the conversation to looking at a more balanced picture of the child. Here is a conversation in which one counselor helped a teacher identify strengths in a child who had been frustrating him for a long time.

> Counselor: Mr. Mosher, you say that Michael always interrupts the class by calling out.
>
> Mr. Mosher: Yes.
>
> Counselor: Is there ever a time when Michael doesn't interrupt?
>
> Mr. Mosher (after thinking a bit): When he is working with another student or in a small group.
>
> Counselor: So, he behaves appropriately in one-on-one or small-group situations. What about those situations might help to keep Michael on task?

After learning about resiliency and strength-based approaches, one counselor reported that she was shocked when she analyzed the negative tone of the conversations in the staff lunchroom and teachers' lounge. Even the front office personnel talked openly and disparagingly about students and their families in front of visitors and other students.

One office manager was heard to say within earshot of several students, staff, and parents, "Oh, here comes Pat with another fake excuse from his hippie mother." Negative conversations about students and families create a pervasively negative atmosphere for everyone in the school. In this situation, the counselor and principal worked together to initiate a plan to improve the professionalism of staff conversations about students and their families. The counselor and principal began consciously modeling positive interactions and reinforcing those that occurred. Among the other steps taken were restructuring faculty meetings to be more positive and presenting information during the meetings about the benefits of focusing on strengths. The faculty was asked to give input on ways to make daily interactions more positive. This was a beginning step in establishing the expectation that everyone would be courteous and respectful in their interactions with others.

Even with students referred for disruptive behavior, school staff can use a strength-based approach when exploring the situation. For example, one school profiled in Chapter 8 changed its office referral forms to reflect an emphasis on students' strengths. Referring teachers were asked not only to identify the offense for which the student was sent to the office, but also the strengths that the student had shown in resolving this type of issue in the past. When counseling a student with behavioral issues, a counselor might begin by eliciting a general description of what occurred, and then say to the student, "I know you don't behave that way all the time. Think of a time when you did not behave in the way that got you in trouble. What were you doing then?" This question helps separate the behavior from the child and also identifies a situation when the child behaved appropriately. From there, the counselor can work collaboratively with the student to identify conditions that produce acceptable behavior, as well as specific actions that the student used when behaving appropriately. This then enables the counselor to commend the child for being

> When counseling a child, particularly a child who has been in your office numerous times, you can gain a new perspective by completing a T-chart (see example on p. 53). On one side, describe all his or her strengths in the situation, such as good sense of humor, concerned family, willing to talk about the situation, good in math and spelling, cooperative on the bus. On the other side, describe the issues or problems. Examination of the T-chart reveals a more balanced picture of the child and facilitates "out of the box" problem solving about ways to change behavior. One counselor regularly used this technique collaboratively with the student. Frequently, the process would lead the student to design his or her own solution to the problem behavior. In another school, the child study team used this procedure for particularly problematic children, involving parents or family members when appropriate.

able to behave as expected. During subsequent interactions, the counselor should look for opportunities to acknowledge and reinforce the student when he or she is behaving appropriately.

Another application of strength-based questioning strategies appears during child study team meetings. Individualized Education Plans (IEPs) are typically developed with a focus on a student's disabilities. When identification of the student's strengths and capabilities is part of the standard IEP process, educators' perceptions about the student frequently change. As part of a program designed to teach child-care providers how to view children based on their abilities and strengths, rather than their deficits, preschool teachers of students with disabilities completed 15 hours of professional development. Prior to this training, staff members described children in terms of their disabilities 42% of the time. Following the training activity, only 10% of the descriptions of children focused on their disabilities (Campbell et al., 2001).

A T-chart is potentially another very effective tool in reorienting educators' perspectives of a student who is struggling academically or behaviorally. The student's strengths are listed in the left-hand column of the chart and his or her problems on the right-hand side. The student is then helped to focus on developing strategies that build on his or her strengths. This process is second nature to successful coaches. They draw on athletes' existing strengths while simultaneously developing areas needing refinement.

T-Chart

STRENGTHS	PROBLEMS
• Good math skills • Volunteers to help • Has a winning smile • Good attendance • Few discipline problems on the bus	• Calling out in class • Interrupts other students who are doing seatwork • Uses profanity in class • Has difficulty working independently • Gets into loud verbal arguments on the playground

Classroom and Small-Group Strength-Based Practices
That Promote Resiliency

As noted in Chapter 1, resiliency is an innate quality of all humans. Emmy Werner (1999) describes it as the self-righting characteristic of the human organism. Resiliency is not something that can be taught. Instead, it is promoted by establishing environments and practices that facilitate individuals in discovering the strengths and resiliency that lie within them. This notion is supported by the work of Bickart and Wolin (1997), who evaluated the Washington, D.C., Project Resilience. They found that the school experiences that fostered resiliency resulted not from specially designed lessons and activities, such as those often used by counselors in their guidance curricula, but from seven key teaching practices listed below. In general, when teachers created opportunities to develop and practice behaviors associated with resiliency during daily interactions and instructions, students displayed more resilient behaviors. Thus, it is not the once-a-week lesson or activity provided by a school counselor but the ongoing reinforcement of resilient characteristics such as insight, independence, relationship building, initiative, creativity, humor, and morality that fosters the development of resiliency.

Bickart and Wolin (1997) identified seven key classroom teaching strategies that promote resiliency:

1. Involving students in assessing their own work and setting goals for themselves.
2. Involving students in developing standards for their work.
3. Offering students many opportunities to work cooperatively.
4. Having students participate in classroom meetings to solve classroom problems.
5. Providing children with opportunities to make choices.
6. Organizing the classroom as a community and promoting student bonding to that community.
7. Encouraging students to play an active role in setting rules for classroom life.

If the classroom is, in fact, the place where resiliency can be most effectively fostered, what then is the role of the school counselor? Within the Comprehensive Guidance Program Model approach discussed in Chapter 5, the counselor would still focus on the four main areas— guidance curriculum, individual planning, responsive services, and systems support. However, shifting to a resiliency-based approach might alter the percentage of time a counselor would spend in each area. For example, a counselor might spend relatively more time in coaching teachers to implement resiliency-promoting strategies and less time teaching guidance lessons in the classroom.

It is still important for counselors to have regular classroom contact with students to teach various aspects of the guidance curriculum. However, given that a resiliency focus shifts attention away from changing individual children and toward creating an environment where all children are naturally nurtured, counselors might allocate some of their classroom time to providing systems support. In this effort, counselors would use their skills of decision making, problem solving, and other pro-social behaviors to assist teachers in creating classroom communities, and involving students in role-playing and negotiations as well as involving them more deeply in their own academic work. For example, at Two Rivers Elementary School, a second-grade teacher was seriously injured in a traffic accident. Realizing that a long-term substitute teacher would have to take over the class, counselor Nancy Harrata met with the class and brainstormed with them how they could best continue their learning with the substitute teacher. They role-played potentially problematic situations and designed a plan to help the new teacher learn about them and their classroom. Making students partially responsible for the success of the transition gave them an investment in supporting rather than undermining the substitute's efforts.

The following section focuses on strategies counselors or teachers can implement in classrooms or with small groups. The examples are organized around a model developed by Henderson and Milstein (1996). Based on a research review, this model identifies six factors that promote resiliency by both mitigating risk factors and increasing protective factors.

Table 6.1 summarizes selected practices that support each of the six factors. From a review of the literature on resiliency, Bonnie Benard (1991) reached conclusions similar to those of Milstein and Henderson. She has identified three major categories of protective processes critical to creating resilient environments: (a) caring and supportive relationships, (b) high expectations, and (c) opportunities for meaningful participation.

Pro-Social Bonding

Pro-social bonding involves strengthening positive connections between a child and institutions, people, or activities. These positive connections between a child and caring adults at a school can diminish the harshness of outside experiences over which the school has no control. There are many ways to increase pro-social bonding and

Table 6.1. Activities Corresponding to Each Component of the Henderson and Milstein (1996) Resiliency Model

MODEL COMPONENT	ACTIVITIES
Pro-social bonding	School pride; welcome ambassadors program; clear, well-communicated vision
Clear, consistent boundaries	Schoolwide behavioral expectations; abundant praise for appropriate behavior; clear definitions of infractions; standard referral process; models of expected behaviors; peer mediation
Meaningful participation	Involvement in rule setting, class meetings, student council, service learning, community service, peer mediation, and peer mentoring
High expectations	Study clubs; tutoring; engaging classroom lessons; academic expectations stated and rewarded often; students given support to meet expectations; homework; praise for effort and progress
Care and concern	Kindness and respect toward all members of the school community; direct and honest feedback and communication
Life skills	Evidence-based curricula; student rewards for good decision making, problem solving, conflict resolution, etc.; opportunities to practice life skills

connectedness to school. Demonstrating trust and respect for students and for all the adults at the school is a starting place. Involving students in activities such as a welcome ambassadors group, buddy group, or class meeting helps them learn to assume responsibility, as well as giving them opportunities to take pride in their contributions to the school.

As an example of creating opportunities for student contributions, on the first day of school, one teacher in an inner-city school with high student mobility asked her students, "What will be the biggest barrier to our learning this year?" The students identified the time the teacher had to take away from instruction when a new student came into the classroom. The students suggested forming a welcoming committee that would take over some of these responsibilities. Each month a new group of children was assigned to the welcoming committee. Whenever new students came into the classroom, the welcoming committee taught them the rules and procedures and helped to integrate them into the class.

Other ways of increasing connections include establishing rituals (such as a special sign that identifies a class) and ceremonies that support academic success and positive social interactions. Sharing visions, values, and expectations are other ways to reinforce pro-social bonding. Positive interactions speak volumes to a student. Perhaps one of the easiest ways of helping students connect to school is through positive interactions with staff and faculty. Bosworth (1995) asked students to identify characteristics of caring teachers. She found that the students identified some simple teacher behaviors: helping with schoolwork, being "nice," and having and expressing high expectations.

Clear and Consistent Boundaries

Clear and consistent boundaries establish consistency and increase students' perceptions that they are treated fairly, regardless of other factors such as socioeconomic status, ethnicity, gender, or English language proficiency. School policies and practices should clarify behavioral expectations and be consistently implemented. Rules are more effective in establishing behavioral expectations if the students know what they should do, rather than what they are prohibited from doing. For example, "Always walk in the hallways," is preferable to "No running in the hallways." Counselors can play an important role in helping students understand why rules exist and why it is important that everyone follows the rules. Modeling expected behaviors reinforces established boundaries, as does regularly praising expected behaviors as they occur. Counselors can assist other personnel in ensuring that developmentally appropriate structures are in place to guide students in understanding boundaries.

Meaningful Participation

Meaningful opportunities for participation provide students with opportunities to solve problems, make decisions, plan, set goals, and help others. Meaningful participation gives students a sense of power and can serve to develop an internal locus of control. It is important to remember that participation is meaningful only if the student views it as such.

Simple tasks such as being a line leader, erasing the board, or passing out papers can be very meaningful to young children, if they are presented as contributions to the classroom. For older students, participation in student advisory groups and school activity planning groups is often a significant experience. Peer mediation programs, cross-age tutoring, and mentoring activities have the dual benefit of providing meaningful participation while reinforcing social and academic skills. Participation in classroom-based decision making and class meetings is another way to give all students a voice in important matters.

As mentioned previously, participation must be meaningful in order to promote resiliency and competencies. The best way to ensure that the student sees value in the experience is to encourage student input. When seeking input, it is particularly important that students understand how their input will be used. For example, if a vote constitutes their input, the results of that vote should be honored in future decision making. If student input is part of a larger process of collecting information to guide decision making—and the student input may not necessarily be acted on—students should be aware of this from the beginning. Students, like adults, feel rejected when they believe their efforts have been ignored.

High Expectations

Having high and clearly communicated expectations for every student's academic and social development is another protective factor. Students have a way of rising (or sinking) to adults' expectations of them. High expectations provide the motivation for students to succeed, and convey a belief in the child's potential and competence. What resiliency research adds to traditional models of high expectations is the recognition that expectations must be accompanied by purposeful support to guide students in attaining them (Krovetz, 1999). Counselors and other educators cannot expect all students to have the skills to achieve high expectations without any assistance or support from adults. For students who may struggle to reach the expectations, it is critical that educators watch for and acknowledge progress in the desired direction. Counselors can play a critical role in helping teachers establish high but attainable expectations as well as provide the support for meeting those expectations.

Care and Concern

A caring, supportive environment is the foundation for academic success. All human beings need caring and support. Children perceive as caring those adults who expect them to do their best, offer assistance when necessary without taking away the task, and celebrate their successes, small and large. Students want to be held accountable to established standards and value teachers who respect them enough to do this. Students also report that caring teachers do not pass on their opinions of a student to the student's next teacher, particularly when those notions are negative (Krovetz, 1999).

Giving praise and providing opportunities to succeed are characteristics of a caring environment. Problem situations present golden opportunities for adults to show caring and support. When they get in trouble, children often fear rejection. A caring adult does not judge or criticize the child as a person. Rather, the adult communicates a clear message that the *behavior* was not appropriate and that the child is capable of doing better. Consequences should be proportionate to the offense and, whenever possible, related to rectifying the situation. For example, having a student who damages property repair or replace it is preferable to a generic punishment such as detention. Discipline is an ideal time to "reteach" or redirect behavior to a student's strengths.

In American schools, praise is often limited in several ways. First, students are typically praised for achievement in either academics or athletics. Students who have talents in other areas generally do not receive the same amount of attention for their accomplishments.

Another characteristic is that the product, not the process, is praised. Thus, students are typically judged (and therefore praised) on completed projects. They receive little praise for successful accomplishment of the many steps that lead up to completion. Without praise and feedback on the process, students may not successfully learn all the steps necessary to complete a project and will continue to have difficulty completing academic projects. The same applies to students who are struggling with behavioral changes. Those students need praise for each step toward a goal, as well as for each time they show restraint or demonstrate desired behavior changes. Expecting the child to demonstrate an entire week of good behavior in order to receive praise, without any feedback in the interim, is unrealistic.

Praise must be specific. Generic statements such as "good job!" or "great work!" do not give a student any information about what specifically was great or good. Without specific feedback on the behavior, the student will have a difficult time replicating the action that was praised. Much more effective is praise that gives students information about what behaviors to increase in order to gain more success. For example, "I really like the way you remembered to show all your work on all the problems" communicates useful, specific feedback to the child.

Safety is a basic need and a necessary condition for a caring and supportive environment. Schools must be safe places for students, both physically and emotionally. The physical environment of a school should be free of avoidable risks and hazards. While this generally is the responsibility of school administrators, counselors and teachers can help students understand the procedures that are in place to keep them safe. School evacuation drills, such as fire drills, should be explained to students and practiced. School lockdown drills should also be developed and practiced to prepare for instances when it is important to keep children safe from outside forces, such as an intruder or crime situation. Too many students live in environments where the outside environment presents safety risks, a fact that cannot be ignored. Practicing evacuation and lockdown drills demonstrates to students that adults are taking care of their basic safety needs. At the same time, adults need to be reassuring that the school is generally a safe place where students do not need to feel afraid.

Environments must be not only physically but also psychologically safe. Students should be free of the fear of bullying, name calling, or harassment. Students should know that if they go to an adult for assistance, that adult will help them. Classrooms, cafeterias, playgrounds, and offices must be free of sarcasm and ridicule. To feel psychologically safe, a student must feel respected.

Life Skills

Integrating into regular daily instruction life skills training that helps students successfully deal with life's challenges is another key component of an environment that promotes student resiliency. Life skills encompass specific behaviors and skills that enable an individual to act effectively and responsibly; examples are conflict resolution, decision making, problem solving, goal setting, and critical thinking. These skills often require direct instruction. Numerous evidence-based curricula and programs are available to provide age-appropriate direct instruction. Before teaching these skills, counselors need to explore these evidence-based resources (see sidebar for resources).

In addition, opportunities to practice these skills should be integrated into ongoing lessons, classroom practices, and school routines whenever possible. Once students have learned these skills, they need opportunities to practice them in both social and academic settings. The counseling staff may be best equipped to help teachers present these skills and identify junctures within the curriculum where these skills can be practiced and applied. Other school personnel who interact with students during the day can also be educated in how to apply life skills in settings such as the cafeteria, library, playground, etc.

To learn certain life skills, such as problem solving or conflict resolution, students require a supportive environment where they feel safe practicing these skills. Cooperation is another critical life skill, particularly with regard to learning to balance autonomy and self-reliance with participation as a member of a community.

The following resources give descriptions and reviews of evidence-based prevention programs and are useful tools in locating effective curricula and programs.

Drug Strategies. (1998). *Safe schools, safe students: A guide to violence prevention strategies.* Washington, D.C.: Author.

Drug Strategies. (1999). *Making the grade: A guide to school drug prevention programs.* Washington, D.C.: Author.

Schinke, S., Brounstein, P., & Gardner, S. (2002). *Science-based prevention programs and principles.* (DHHS Pub. No. [SMA] 03-3764). Rockville, MD: Center for Substance Abuse Prevention, Substance Abuse and Mental Health Services Administration.

U.S. Department of Education, Safe, Disciplined, and Drug-Free Schools Expert Panel. (2001). *Exemplary and promising safe, disciplined, and drug-free schools programs.* Washington, D.C.: U.S. Department of Education.

Conclusion

As presented in this chapter, there are numerous counselor activities that promote resiliency. Many of these focus on working with individual children, small groups, or classrooms. The next chapter focuses on schoolwide practices.

Chapter 7

Implementing a Schoolwide Resiliency Program[*]

The previous chapter provided strategies that counselors can implement to introduce changes and resiliency-enhancing practices to a school while remaining within their traditional role. In this chapter, we will focus on how counselors can be active in the process of schoolwide change.

The Case for Going Schoolwide

Resiliency is an important concept because it enables caring adults to focus on the strengths, or assets, present in children, their families, and their environments, rather than focusing on what is wrong with them. Another promising feature is that incorporating resiliency-enhancing features into settings such as counseling groups, classrooms, or entire schools can benefit all children, not just those with specific, identified deficits or problems. Installing resiliency concepts at an environmental level necessitates rethinking the culture, policies, and procedures of the school. But once the changes are in place, they can be maintained with much less time and effort than it takes to test, analyze, and label children, and pull them out for special services. This frees up extra time and resources for those children with severe problems who need help the most.

A team of researchers from Howard University and Johns Hopkins University examined how schools affected academic success of poor and minority students (Borman & Rachuba, 2001). The sample included 925 poor, ethnically diverse students in the third grade. They found the strongest predictor of academic success among these students was student engagement in learning, followed by internal locus of control, self-efficacy in math, positive attitude toward school, and self-esteem. The authors concluded that "the most powerful models for promoting [academic] resiliency appear to be those elements that actively shield children from adversity" (p. 20). In addition, they report, "We find that attentiveness to the psychosocial adjustment and school engagement of academically at-risk students are the keys to academic resilience" (p. 21).

School personnel can play a significant role in the success of a child. Emmy Werner (1999) found that educators are second only to the immediate family in positively influencing the lives of resilient children. Especially for children who grow up in adverse or high-stress conditions, educators may have profound impacts on their lives beyond the realm of academic subjects (Zimmerman, 1994). Often, school personnel may have a powerful effect on an individual child without realizing it.

Protective Schools

Depending on its quality, the school experience can become either a risk factor or a protective factor buffering the effects of negative influences in the home, the community, or the biological and psychological makeup of the child. Thus, the school becomes not merely a site for the presentation of a prevention curriculum or "add-on" intervention, but a place where negative behaviors are prevented by the inherent nature of everyday policies and interactions at the school. Based on an expert panel, review of the literature, and focus groups with community members, teachers, school administrators, and educational policymakers, Bosworth (2000) identified 10 characteristics of a protective school environment. While each of these 10 elements can be focused on preventing negative developmental outcomes for students, they also are characteristic of schools with strong academic programs and the resources needed to support student academic success. Thus, in a *protective school,* the lines between what is prevention and what is academic reform are blurred, allowing administrators and prevention specialists to work together in a comprehensive program that will support continual healthy development of students (Bosworth, 2000). See www.protectiveschools.org for a copy of *Protective Schools.*

The interconnecting characteristics of a protective school are as follows:

1. A vision of success that has broad community support
2. A healthy school culture so that students bond to school

3. The commitment and engagement of school leaders to prevention and school reform activities
4. A strong academic program that promotes student success
5. Implementation of effective prevention curricula or programs
6. Integration of prevention and intervention efforts into a continuum of strategies and services
7. Ongoing professional development to support and maintain an effective and empowered faculty and staff
8. Strong home, school, and community relationships
9. Mobilization and leveraging of funding and resources for prevention
10. Regular collection and analysis of data to guide decision making

A Protective Schools planning process has been developed for several elementary school counselors through a federal grant (Project CLEAR). In their first week at their schools, the Project CLEAR counselors interviewed school personnel and observed the school environment to identify the school's strengths and opportunities for change in terms of the 10 characteristics. Later the entire group of CLEAR counselors met to discuss their observations and assessment results. Each then identified three Protective School areas to work on in the coming school year. They then met with the school principal to negotiate goals and objectives, timelines, and resource requirements necessary for implementation. One counselor used faculty meetings to take the faculty through a visioning process. Another counselor revived use of an evidence-based violence prevention program by providing staff development on the curriculum and then co-teaching initial lessons. In another school the counselor organized schoolwide assemblies for the purpose of praising and awarding individual students, as well as classroom procedures and clubs for acknowledging progress and success.

Another group of schools is implementing the Protective Schools model through a more formal process that includes a faculty-wide needs assessment, a faculty brainstorming meeting, and development of a three-year action plan. This process from the LINKS (Linking Interventions and Networks for Kids and Schools) project (A Safe Schools/Healthy Students project) will be described in full later in the chapter.

Schoolwide Practices That Promote Resiliency

Protective Environments—Evidence-Based Practices

The power of protective factors in fostering resiliency among children, especially those youngsters who grow up under adverse circumstances, has been well documented. Little can be done in school settings to alter individual characteristics, such as intelligence and temperament, or family characteristics, such as alcoholism or violence. Given these limitations, the question for school personnel is, "How can the school environment support healthy growth and development?"

Michael Rutter and his colleagues (1979) examined the impact that schools had on children from an impoverished area of London. During the middle school years, various school characteristics had profound positive or negative consequences for four outcome variables: achievement scores, delinquency, student behavior, and attendance. The results indicated that positive outcomes clustered in those schools that had high achievement, high attendance, positive student behavior, and low levels of delinquency. Those schools that had low achievement scores reported poor attendance, more disruptive student behavior, and higher levels of delinquency.

Specifically Rutter and colleagues (1979) concluded that "children's academic attainment was also strongly and consistently associated with school process influences, even after other variables had been statistically [taken] into account" (p.175). The correlations between developmental outcomes and school characteristics remained reasonably stable for at least five years. In other words, the impact of a "good" school on student outcomes can continue even after the student has left that school.

The researchers reported that the differences between high-achieving and low-achieving schools were not due to physical factors, such as the size of the school, the age of the buildings, or the available space. They also were not attributable to differences in administrative structure, organization, or gender mix (same-sex versus coeducational). Rather, the differences were related to the schools' characteristics as social institutions in terms of the overall quality of relationships and emotional climate.

Specific characteristics defined the successful schools. These included strong academic emphasis, frequent availability of incentives and rewards, good physical condition of the school, opportunities for students to have meaningful roles and responsibilities, and specific teacher classroom management practices, such as starting class on time and having clear lesson plans. Teachers conveyed the value of education in part by taking good care of the building and the classrooms. The adults in the school modeled positive behaviors for students. Outcomes tended to be better when there was widespread support and agreement among the staff regarding the curriculum and approaches to discipline. Importantly, higher exam scores and lower delinquency rates occurred in schools where discipline was based on general schoolwide expectations rather than being left to individual teachers. Participation was another key factor in differentiating the schools. Teachers in the successful schools reported feeling that they played a part in the decision-making process and had confidence in the staff as a whole to make good decisions for the school.

Several very clear implications emerge from this research. Students who overcome adversity are neither flukes nor exceptionally talented. Clear processes that exist within the student's environment foster positive growth and development. These processes can be adapted and integrated into existing environments to provide protective factors that will buffer students from adversity.

Changing the School Environment to Promote Resiliency in Students

To summarize, research clearly indicates that most children born into adverse or high-stress situations are able to rise above those situations and be successful. There is also evidence that conditions in the school environment can have a positive influence on students from adverse home, family, and community backgrounds. The final question is whether systematically modifying the school environment can make a difference in children's outcomes. Several researchers have demonstrated that environmental modification does make a difference.

Multimodal School-Based Prevention Demonstration Project

The Multimodal School-Based Prevention Demonstration Project (Gottfredson, Gottfredson, & Skroban, 1996) was a multi-component intervention for middle school students designed to foster academic achievement, social competency in development, and social bonding. The project components included using cooperative learning techniques and one-on-one tutoring to improve instruction, providing social support, providing mentoring for high-risk students, and teaching cognitive-behavioral skills through a 16-session course called Life Skills Training. At the end of four years of implementation, high-risk youth showed significant positive changes in grade point average and reduction of peer drug influence.

Good Behavior Game

Kellam and colleagues (1998) introduced a team-based behavior management strategy called the Good Behavior Game. This strategy promotes pro-social behavior by rewarding teams of students whose members do not exhibit any maladaptive behaviors during precisely defined periods. First-grade teachers were taught how to implement the Good Behavior Game by rewarding short periods of positive classroom behavior. The length of time required to earn a reward for team behavior gradually increased over an academic year until these behavioral expectations became part of the general management of the classroom. In a longitudinal evaluation, Kellam and colleagues discovered that among boys who displayed the highest level of aggression in the first grade, those that were in classrooms not implementing the Good Behavior Game were 59 times more likely to be rated as highly aggressive in middle school than were those who were in classrooms implementing the Good Behavior Game.

Positive Behavior Support

Positive Behavior Support (PBS) is an application of behavioral research to educational practice designed to enhance the school environment. Within the PBS system, attention is focused on creating and sustaining school environments that promote positive lifestyle results for all children by making problem behavior less effective, efficient, and relevant while making pro-social behavior more functional. Features of a school that has adopted a PBS approach include practices in which (a) primary prevention is a priority and is visible schoolwide, and (b) positive behavioral expectations are defined, taught, and encouraged schoolwide for all students and staff. A number of rigorously conducted studies have indicated that office discipline referrals decrease dramatically and that, as the behavioral culture of the school improves, so do behavior and academic performance (Carr et al., 1999; Sugai et al., 2000).

A resiliency approach that is grounded in strength-based attitudes and perspectives provides direction to a counselor's work. This focus is appropriate whether the counselor is providing a classroom lesson or teaching teachers how to implement an evidence-based violence prevention curriculum.

Organizational Change

Change within an organization may take place at many levels. For example, one teacher may learn about resiliency and decide to change the practices and management in his or her particular classroom. A single counselor may opt to use strength-based approaches when counseling individual students or groups of students or presenting a guidance lesson to a class. Introducing the concept of resiliency into an entire school, however, presents more challenges because it necessitates systemic change.

Whether at the individual or schoolwide level, the change process is not linear and requires continual review of progress and revision of plans. Knowing how to change a situation is an entirely different matter from actually changing it. For example, after it was discovered that supplementing a sailor's diet with citrus fruit would prevent scurvy, it took more than 100 years to put this seemingly straightforward prevention into common practice. Successful change efforts require at least three things: (a) a commitment to the change, (b) an understanding of the change process, and (c) a plan for change.

Clearly one of the biggest challenges in the integration of any change into an organization is its actual implementation. Those guiding implementation need to understand the dynamics of how organizations and human beings respond when confronted with change; the role of leadership in organizing a process for implementing change; and the steps involved in planning the change, taking action, and evaluating the outcomes.

The Dynamics of Organizations and Change

A systems approach is helpful in understanding why change is difficult to institutionalize. Most management systems have their roots in the "scientific management" techniques developed during the Industrial Revolution. A metaphor commonly used for such a system is the "factory model." The factory model embraces three assumptions: (a) management and labor are separate and work together mostly in a system based on rigid roles and exchange of services; (b) production is an automated, mechanical process, thus work and workers are also mechanical processes; and (c) like a broken part on a machine, a worker can be replaced and the system will still function.

In a school, this approach manifests itself in top-down leadership, with the principal directing faculty and staff, and faculty directing the learning of students. Curriculum is standardized, so the content taught in freshman English class is essentially the same, regardless of which teacher teaches the course. Students are viewed as having deficits in knowledge, which the teachers fix by giving students the knowledge and skills they lack. Whereas the factory model may have been reasonably efficient for education in the industrial era, it does not fit with contemporary research on how children learn best nor with the multiple demands placed on today's schools. It ignores one critical, undeniable element: Neither teachers nor students are machines. They are living beings. As such, mechanical approaches have limitations, particularly when change happens as quickly as it does in the twenty-first century.

Organizations are living, organic systems, just as the people who comprise them are. Margaret Wheatley, in *Leadership and the New Science* (1999), reports that a key characteristic of a living system is the "extraordinary capacity to change, to adapt, and to grow as required" (p. xvi). A living systems approach recognizes that bringing change to individuals and organizations is not as simple as removing an old part and installing a new one. Like any other living system, individuals and organizations need nourishment and proper environmental conditions to grow, develop, and thrive.

Thus, a change imposed from outside, even an inherently valuable one, is unlikely to be maintained. Most counselors can recall an experience where a sound, evidence-based program was implemented in their school through a grant or an outside funding source. While funding was available, implementation was successful. But shortly after the financial support was decreased or terminated, the school abandoned the program (see, e.g., DeJong & Moegkens, 1995; Kelder et al., 1996; Lieber & Civitas, 1994; Nadel, Spellman, & Alvarez-Canino, 1996; Swisher, 2000; Wiist, Jackson, & Jackson, 1996).

A living systems perspective reminds us to take the needs of the entire system into account when planning change. Accordingly, Deevy (1995) and Quinn, Greunert, and Valentine (1999) advocate that an organization's culture must change before employees' behavior will change. Oakley and Krug (1991) suggest that leaders must consider people's mindsets before attempting systemic change. Individuals' mindsets and spirits are critical to any organizational improvement effort because employees have to be willing to risk change and contribute to the process. Traditional command-and-control management systems have created deep-seated dependency among employees (Deevy, 1995). The management-versus-labor, or us-versus-them, mentality that results from top-down management practices leaves employees unwilling to assume personal risk and responsibility. For many employees, this dependency relationship has led to poor self-image and self-esteem. They may interpret requests or mandates to change as implying that something is wrong with them, which leads to defensive, self-protective resistance to change (Oakley & Krug, 1991). This dynamic exists among many teachers. They may perceive change efforts as indicating that they are considered incompetent, or that their way of doing things is being rejected, even though they believe they are doing the right things (Quinn et al., 1999).

Critical to implementing a resiliency program (or any other program or process) is to view the school as a living system rather than a factory. As such, each school has characteristics in common with all other living systems, but also has unique needs. All living systems need to be fed and nourished to survive. Dog food nourishes a beagle, but not a houseplant or a goldfish. In the same way, no one approach for enhancing resiliency is effective for all children. Counselors wishing to introduce resiliency-enhancing practices need to select programs and practices that have a high likelihood of succeeding with the students in their particular school. Thus, programs and practices need to match with the culture of the school, be age-appropriate, and have documented evidence of effectiveness.

Once a specific program or set of practices is selected, the next job is to analyze how the subsystems in the school function. A major focus of the analysis should be a review of the school's history with change. What changes have been successful and which ones are still in place? What factors led to their success? Equally important is to examine the changes or innovations that were unsuccessful and the factors that accounted for their not becoming institutionalized. Through this institutional analysis, those forces that promote change and those that impede it can be identified and carefully taken into consideration when planning what to change and how to introduce the change.

For example, six years ago at Riverdale Middle School, the counselor, Ken Renaldi, introduced a peer mediation program. Some students and some teachers became involved, but after two years, Ken decided that the effort was not paying off and dropped the program. Now that the staff at Riverdale is looking to implement universal schoolwide violence prevention, Ken has reviewed his ideas on why the peer mediation program did not become institutionalized. He concluded the following:

1. The program did not have the support of the principal.
2. No professional development on the benefits of the program was provided.
3. Only a handful of students were trained.
4. The students trained as mediators were students with clean discipline records and good grades, not school leaders.

This analysis gave Ken clues about ways to increase the likelihood of successful implementation of this new program.

The Dynamics of Human Nature and Change

Any innovation must resonate with the individuals involved. As Oakley and Krug (1991, p. 72) phrase it, "People don't resist change as much as they resist being changed." Deevy (1995) found that historically one of the major impediments to change has been a failure to consider the human dimension. This is consistent with Oakley and Krug's (1991) finding that most workplaces focus on systems and processes, not the human factor. When implementation of a program or change requires the participation of many individuals, the belief systems of these individuals must be blended with the beliefs and values of the organizations of which they are members. No matter what the program or process, individuals will "take *our* work and recreate it as *their* own" (Wheatley & Kellner-Rogers, 1998, p. 8). This means that the members—not just the leaders—of an organization must be involved if a change is to produce desired results. Wheatley and Kellner-Rogers also caution that "we ignore people's need to participate at our own peril" (p. 8).

The human element is a crucial factor in change. People will change when they feel a need to change, when they feel supported and respected, when change moves from the general to the specific, when there is a shift from old ties to new ties, or when they move from an external to an internal commitment to change (Oakley & Krug, 1991; Quinn et al., 1999). What, then, can be done to elicit an interest and willingness to change?

Those who will be implementing the innovation need to feel ownership of the process, rather than feeling that the change is happening *to* them (Blanchard & Waghorn, 1997; Kelder et al., 1996; Schwann & Spady, 1998). They must be meaningfully involved in the change process, which requires access to data and information (Quinn et al., 1999). As Blanchard and Waghorn (1997, p. 69) remind counselors, "If you want everyone to have an ownership stake in the change process you must expose them to all the available information." Moreover, change will not be sustained unless it is clearly linked to the vision, values, and purposes of the people within the organization. Finally, professionals must be willing to grow, work together as a team, and participate in ongoing professional development opportunities aimed at incorporating the change into the culture of the organization.

The Role of Leadership in Change

Leadership support is imperative from the initial stages of

implementation through full incorporation of the innovation. After studying educational reforms in several situations, Fullan (1999) concluded that change is nonlinear and complex. It cannot be the purview of one individual. The role of the principal in school reform is to manage the change within the living system of the school and continually to articulate the vision to the faculty and staff. All parts of the living system must work together, and the principal's responsibility is to direct the growth in consistent directions so efforts are not fragmentary and contradictory.

Ways for leaders to show support for an innovation include establishing a climate of trust, being visible in activities supporting the program, providing resource support, and making the innovation a priority. For any innovation to be successfully adopted, it must be integrated into the culture of the organization and be adaptable to the circumstances of the school (Felner, Favazza, Shim, Brand, Gu, & Noonan, 2001; Moren & Collins, 2000; Nickols, 2000; Schwann & Spady, 1998; Swisher, 2000).

Not all changes supported by school leaders are successfully implemented. Bosworth and colleagues reported that if the change is one of three to five priorities for the leader, then the change is more likely to be successful (Bosworth, Gingiss, Pottoff, & Roberts-Gray, 1999). If the leader has more than five priorities, then there is a good chance that none of the initiatives will be successful, because the leader's time is too scattered. Furthermore, if the leader involves others in the school in the planning and implementation process, the chances for success increase.

Although the principal is the designated leader in a school, counselors play important leadership and advocacy roles. Change can start with the counselor and spread to many in the school in a relatively short period of time, provided that the change process is not forced upon individuals, but rather is presented as an option to be accepted and embraced on an individual basis. In this scenario, counselors are advocates for what they believe. Their interest takes root and sends out runners, which take root and send out more runners, which take root, and so on, until what was a single blade of grass covers a wide area.

For example, one school counselor attended a session on resiliency at a state association conference. He recognized that the concept meshed with many things already happening at his school but could see opportunities to strengthen several other areas through the application of resiliency. Upon returning to his school, he had a long discussion with the principal and gave her some material to read. He wrote about resiliency in his column in the parent newsletter and distributed information at faculty meetings. The principal provided financial support for five faculty members to attend a local conference on resiliency. When they returned expressing enthusiasm about integrating resiliency into their school, the principal announced that she supported joining a collaborative group of schools interested in creating resilient environments. Although this decision could not have been made without the principal's leadership, the counselor played a pivotal leadership role in introducing the concept and disseminating information.

Rogers (1995) identifies five steps necessary to take an innovation or change from the idea stage to full integration: knowledge, persuasion, decision, action, and integration. Before deciding to adopt a resiliency focus, faculty and staff need to have *knowledge* about resiliency and be *persuaded* that this approach will meet their school's goals. *Decisions* may be made in several ways: by consensus, through a democratic process, or by administrators. Decisions that are made with involvement from the majority of the stakeholders have the best chance for successful implementation. Once the adoption decision has been made, then the school community must organize to implement (put into *action*) the strategies. The goal is to *integrate* resiliency into the culture of the school. Research indicates that most organizations need three to five years to move through the process to full integration.

Change usually does not happen without planning. In orchestrating the change process, leaders need to engage in three specific activities: planning, action, and evaluation. The following sections describe each of these activities.

Planning the Change

Most counselors have been involved in projects or innovations that failed because insufficient time was given to planning. They probably also have experienced projects that were never implemented because too much time was spent in planning, while time, funds, or perhaps motivation ran out. Counselors can take the lead in organizing a planning process that provides all stakeholders with the time necessary to think through all aspects of the implementation yet not get bogged down in details. Including the following steps in the planning process for successful implementation can help achieve the balance.

Organizing a Planning Group
Planning and implementing schoolwide change requires the time, skills, and resources of many people in the school. Some schools already have a strategic planning committee or school climate committee, which would be the ideal group to spearhead the adoption of resiliency-based approaches. Other schools may need to create such a working group,

planning committee, or core team. Members of this group need to be representative of the school population in terms of race, gender, grade level, and specialty. One school made the mistake of not including any special education teachers on its planning committee. Because they were excluded from the planning process, the special education teachers did not receive information about the change or how it would benefit them, so they actively opposed it. Several months were lost in getting this school's planning process back on track.

While it is important that the working committee be representative, a relatively small group is best, between five and nine members, because larger groups tend to be inefficient. An administrator and a counselor are essential members. Other interested staff, such as the librarian, the nurse, office staff, the school resource officer, or parent volunteers may be considered as potential members and allies. In order to become advocates for the change and the change process, group members must be knowledgeable about resiliency and the dynamics of change. For this reason, providing training for the group is essential. The group must also make a commitment to meet regularly for planning.

Securing Commitment From Stakeholders

An analysis of the living systems in the school (discussed previously) is an important first step in deciding how best to gain widespread support and commitment from stakeholders (i.e., those who will be affected by the change). Here are two examples of ways to enlist support. One is to gauge faculty and staff support via an anonymous ballot; for example, developers of a three-year grant to support the development of a resiliency climate required 80% support from faculty before accepting a school to participate. In another case, a principal wanted to implement a strategy for class meetings. She recruited the teacher-leaders in her school to pilot the program she felt best suited to the school. These teachers were very supportive of the program based on their experience. The enthusiastic support of these respected teachers convinced even the most reluctant teachers to participate.

Assessment

Understanding the baseline situation is a critical step in the change process. Sometimes on initial review, the situation may seem clear, but input from other perspectives and stakeholders may lead to different conclusions. Whether via informal or formal assessment, it is essential to thoughtfully assess the situation before plunging into action. Counselors are skilled at determining underlying strengths and needs. Those skills can be applied to planning a schoolwide intervention.

Educators participating in the LINKS project complete a formal assessment process using a 30-item questionnaire based on the 10 characteristics of a Protective School. The questionnaire can be completed on the Internet for ease of administration. Once a majority of the faculty have completed the questionnaire, the answers are compiled and reviewed by a planning team at the school to identify strengths and areas of weakness. Once the areas that responding faculty see as most critical have been identified, input from the entire faculty, and, at the principal's discretion, selected staff is solicited.

Involving the Faculty in Planning

In a strength-based planning approach, asking the right questions is essential. Questions that focus on solutions, rather than the reasons a problem exists, are forward focused and thus generate creative thinking rather than reactive thinking. Oakley and Krug (1991, p. 138) call the type of questions used to create a forward focus "effective questions." Effective questions reduce defensiveness by avoiding blame, prompting people to think, empowering individuals to discover their strengths and talents, and helping determine what is needed to get to the desired future. Effective questions also encourage people to take risks, connect personal needs with organizational needs, and create a high-energy, high-trust environment.

Questions that invite discussion are open-ended rather than yes–no in format. Also important is the use of "what" or "how" questions, rather than "why" or "who" questions (Oakley & Krug, 1991). The first two types of questions lower resistance and seek information and opinions rather than explanations. The latter types of questions tend to be perceived as posing a challenge and often heighten defensiveness.

On a broader scale, effective questions can facilitate analysis of a problem affecting a group or organization. For example, an associate superintendent began seeking a new approach when she was assigned the division in the district that had the lowest morale and greatest number of union grievances. To begin focusing on change, she adapted questions from Oakley and Krug's *Framework for Continuous Renewal* (1991). During a series of staff meetings, all staff members of the division were asked to answer the following questions in small groups:

1. What is already working?
2. What makes those things work?
3. What are our objectives?
4. What can we do to move closer to our objectives?

Initially, it was difficult to get staff to identify what was working because they were so accustomed to being told what was wrong. She found that once that barrier was eliminated, creative ideas began to flow. The staff was able to develop a plan that guided them through the entire year. By the end of the year, staff morale was at an all-time high and turnover was the lowest it had been in 10 years. Staff members became enthusiastic participants in developing plans to improve their department. Focusing on the strengths of the division and its employees, and developing goals to build upon those strengths, led to improved climate and morale, a more than two-year hiatus in grievances, and an overall increase in productivity (K. Frey, personal communication, 2000).

In LINKS schools, a faculty brainstorming session is conducted using this effective questions approach. The results are shared with the planning team, which prioritizes the potential activities and examines their goals and resources. The team then creates an action plan to guide the implementation process.

Creating an Action Plan

Following a strength-based planning process, the planning team identifies two to four areas for attention in the coming year and further refines those areas into an action plan. The action plan has specific goals and activities to reach those goals. Timelines and responsible parties are identified, as is a process for monitoring implementation and evaluating progress.

Taking Action

With an action plan that identifies specific tasks, timelines, and responsible parties, implementation can begin. To facilitate successful implementation, someone has to be responsible for monitoring the process. A standard procedure for two-way communication between the planning team and the faculty and administration is also important. This avenue enables the planning committee to share what it is doing with the other staff and receive feedback about new ideas as well as problems that arise during implementation.

As any program is implemented, those responsible for implementation will require additional training, coaching, and support. In one school, counselor Pat Versaci introduced class meetings as a way of increasing meaningful participation and teaching social skills among students. Pat received training in a model for using class meetings (Developmental Studies Center, 2002), then trained all the teachers in the model. As one teacher commented, "The idea seemed very straightforward. After the first class meeting with my students, I had a million questions for Pat!" To help answer routine questions and provide support for the change, Pat held a meeting every Tuesday before school that was open to any teacher who wished to attend. These meetings helped Pat understand the teachers' concerns while giving her an avenue to build trust. At first, only a few teachers came with questions or to share ideas. After several weeks, a core group of teachers became regulars at these sessions, receiving the coaching and support they needed to implement the practice effectively. Others would drop in periodically, especially when they had a question or concern. In addition to this informal support and coaching, several teachers elected to participate in additional training the following summer. When the success of these class meetings became known in the district, Pat and some of the participating teachers were asked to present their program at a district-wide professional development day.

Evaluating Outcomes

Each activity that is completed in the implementation process offers opportunities to identify areas for improvement. For example, in one school, the plan included establishing a student Peace Council to monitor school climate and offer an avenue for meaningful student participation. Initially, one Peace Council representative was elected from each home room. At the first Peace Council meeting, the adult sponsors realized that 90% of the representatives were girls. The next semester, election procedures were changed such that both a male and a female representative were elected from each home room, to achieve a more equitable gender balance.

The responsibility for monitoring and evaluation most appropriately falls on the shoulders of the planning committee. In many schools the counselor plays a key role. An example of counselor monitoring comes from Annice Kim. This counselor introduced an evidence-based violence prevention curriculum designed to teach life skills to her urban middle school students. With input from the principal and several key teachers, she identified faculty at each grade level to receive training in this curriculum. Annice taught or co-taught demonstration lessons initially. As the teachers gained more confidence, she provided advice and monitored their adherence to the written curriculum. When she noticed that some teachers were having difficulty with the role-playing component of the curriculum, she worked with all the teachers to improve their skill and comfort level with this technique.

Careful monitoring is essential in identifying how to improve implementation. A process evaluation makes it possible to identify and correct problems promptly, before they sabotage the implementation process. Periodic review of goals and activities is necessary if the innovation or change is to become fully integrated into the fabric of the organization. In most cases, because of careful monitoring and revisions, the implemented process or program will look different from how it was initially envisioned, which is the nature of living systems.

Conclusion

Introducing any change or innovation is rarely easy. Inevitably different people will have different degrees of enthusiasm for change. Some may feel skeptical because of past negative experiences with failed change, others may feel their current practice does not need to change, and still others may have burned out, losing their original passion for influencing children's lives. Most, however, welcome guidance that will help them to make an important difference in another human being's life. The vision has always been present; the tools are now here. Counselors may be the professionals best situated to become the change agents who will introduce resiliency into the beliefs, attitudes, and behaviors of everyone in their schools.

---

*With contributions from Katie Frey, Ph.D.

Chapter 8

Resiliency in Action:
Exemplary Models of Effective Practices
and Programs*

The fact that many, if not most, children born into adverse or high-stress environments are successful in life, and that schools can facilitate that success, is clearly indicated by resiliency research (Werner & Smith, 1982, 1992). As the examples in the preceding chapters illustrate, many counselors and other educators have been translating principles of resiliency into practice in their schools. Many of these successful efforts have been based on Everett Rogers' (1995) five-stage model of the implementation process, outlined in Chapter 7. (Recall that the five stages are knowledge, persuasion, decision, action, and integration.) This chapter focuses on the stories of counselors who played pivotal roles in the successful implementation of resiliency programs at their sites.

At Independence High School, counselor Teresa Bell and her principal, Dr. Frances Davos, teamed up to create a more positive work environment for faculty and staff based on resiliency principles. At Jefferson Elementary School, counselor Maria Telles led a team of teachers in redesigning practice to promote a more resilient climate for students. At Mountain Vista, a middle school threatened by violence, counselor Carrie Jimenez introduced an evidence-based violence prevention curriculum. And finally, counselors Jim Downey at Randall Elementary School and Tammy Ikeda at Harris Elementary School worked together to organize a joint peace march and conference.

Independence High School

Independence High School, with 1,800 students, is one of four high schools in a moderate-sized city located about 40 miles from a major industrial city in the Midwest. The student body draws from a spectrum of the city's population, including middle-class suburbs, a rural area, Section 8 housing, and the inner city, which has traditionally housed low-income and working-class African Americans. A recent influx of immigrants from the former Soviet Union has dramatically increased the number of limited-English-proficient students over the past several years. The faculty is stable and professional. The principal has been at the school for 10 years and worked with the lead counselor, Teresa Bell, at her previous school.

Anyone who knows Teresa Bell recognizes her optimistic view of the world. She is a strong advocate for children, especially the low-income children that constitute many of the students at Independence High School. Several years ago, Teresa saw a flyer for a conference on resiliency in a nearby city and decided to attend. The conference speakers inspired her, and she was pleased to be able to talk with others who shared her enthusiasm. She met a number of educators who were implementing resiliency-based practices in their schools. This experience piqued her interest in exploring the topic further. Teresa searched the Internet, identified different sources of information, wrote a summary of all she found for her principal, and created the fact sheet displayed at the end of this chapter.

The principal, Dr. Davos, had recently completed her doctoral studies and was anxious to apply research-based practices in the school. What impressed her about resiliency was the evidence of a positive relationship between school climate and academic functioning. Because most of the material Teresa had been able to locate focused on elementary and middle school, she asked to meet with her to discuss this information further and to strategize how the principles of resilience might be practiced at Independence. Together they explored how the three core concepts of care and concern, meaningful participation, and high expectations (Benard, 1991) might be operationalized in a large urban high school. A few weeks after they had begun meeting, a conflict between the English and social studies departments over space allocation erupted into several heated, emotional debates in faculty meetings. Accusations and recriminations flew back and forth. Neither side was able to set aside its position long enough to begin problem solving. Dr. Davos ended the confrontation by making an executive decision about how space would be allocated, but the experience left her convinced that the faculty themselves needed more resiliency before they could support and encourage resiliency in students.

In talking about the situation, both Teresa and Dr. Davos realized that the faculty typically worked in isolation. This isolation fed into feelings of not being valued and suspiciousness of other faculty and the administration, so building faculty resiliency was necessary before resiliency principles could be transferred to the students. Therefore, Dr. Davos asked Teresa to lead a working group of faculty to explore ways to create a stronger sense of belonging and a more productive work environment for faculty. Over the next two months, this team, consisting of one teacher from each department plus the librarian, learned about the concepts of resiliency, read and discussed research on resiliency and school climate, and brainstormed ways to be more supportive of each other. The proposal they presented to Dr. Davos included these recommendations:

1. Creating faculty study groups on resiliency and school climate. Participation would be voluntary but would earn professional development credit.
2. Faculty brainstorming on ways to enhance professionalism in the faculty.
3. Provision of resources for activities generated from the faculty brainstorming.
4. More demonstrations of positive support and encouragement from administration.

At the faculty retreat before the next semester, the team led a brainstorming session with the entire faculty, utilizing the series of questions presented in Chapter 7 (What is working? What makes it work? What are our goals? What can we do to reach the goals?). From this brainstorming session emerged several areas for further action:

1. Provide more opportunities for social interaction among faculty.
2. Provide time for cross-disciplinary faculty discussions about teaching and learning research and issues.
3. Give faculty a greater role in the budget and decision-making processes in the school.

Three committees were formed, each charged with identifying specific action steps to implement one goal. Each committee contained members from every department and representatives from other certified staff. Teresa was given the responsibility of coordinating and monitoring the activities of the three committees. Following are some of the activities that were initiated the following year.

1. A schedule for professional development was posted that included a monthly cross-department discussion of teaching and learning.
2. At one faculty meeting per month, birthdays for that month were celebrated.
3. Dr. Davos hosted monthly dinners at her home, inviting a different group of faculty each time. By the end of the year, all faculty members and professional staff had been included.
4. Teresa led two study groups for which faculty received district credit. One was on resiliency and the other focused on current educational practices.
5. A "kudos" white board was placed in the faculty lounge so faculty could write messages of gratitude and appreciation to each other.
6. A faculty budget committee was established, and members negotiated with Dr. Davos to create a meaningful role for it within the parameters of district policy.

A year after these changes were established, the district lost a bond referendum. Because of the resulting financial strain, the superintendent requested that all schools develop a plan for operating on decreased revenue. Not only was Independence High School the first district school to have a new fiscal plan in place, but school staff received praise for their high morale and positive attitude during this stressful time. Both Teresa and Dr. Davos credited the climate of resiliency among the faculty as a major factor in their successful transition. The nurturing climate served as a buffer against the stress of the ongoing changes. As Teresa explained, "Other schools saw this as a crisis; we had things set up so our committees responded to it as a challenge."

Jefferson Elementary School

Jefferson Elementary School is located in a transitional neighborhood in a large Southwestern city. The children who walk to school are from third- and fourth-generation Hispanic families who have lived in the neighborhood for years. Another group of children is bussed in from transient housing, and a smaller number of students is bussed in from a new middle-class housing development. Several years ago, counselor Maria Telles and a few Jefferson teachers attended a workshop on resiliency in a city several hours away. In the car on the way home, they discussed how they might implement the concepts of resiliency at Jefferson. The remainder of this section describes the three-year process that evolved for integrating resiliency concepts into the culture at Jefferson.

Initially, the group of teachers who attended the workshop, with the support of the counselor, began to try out some of the ideas in their classrooms. As they saw positive results, they shared their experiences with their grade level and department colleagues. Some shared this information with the principal, Maurice Caine. Although supportive of the concept of resiliency, Mr. Caine reminded the staff members that raising academic achievement scores must be the first priority at Jefferson. The resiliency advocates stepped back and examined what if any impact their introduction of resiliency practices had had on achievement. Noticing no negative effects on achievement and seeing more positive attitudes in their classrooms, they continued modifying their practice. The word spread and more teachers gained interest. Mr. Caine recognized the positive changes in the classrooms and began exploring ways in which schoolwide activities might expand the impact.

The following year, Mr. Caine and Maria organized professional development activities centered on actions staff members could take to create environments that foster social and academic success for all students. Some staff members accepted the resiliency focus easily. Others adopted a wait-and-see attitude. Still others adamantly resisted the change and transferred to other schools at the end of the year. On the whole, however, resiliency resonated with faculty beliefs, attitudes, and assumptions. The resiliency advocates persevered, recruiting additional colleagues along the way. They were able to insert a study of resiliency into the school's annual plan.

Toward the end of the school year, when the goal planning process for the next year began, several resiliency advocates were members of the planning group. Ultimately, the planning group decided that a schoolwide resiliency approach should be studied during the next school year. As part of this effort, speakers were brought in during the following school year and research on resiliency was studied. The counselor and core groups of teachers also shared their positive experiences. By the end of the year, the principal, staff, and planning group agreed that a resiliency focus fit with the mission and vision of the school. They were persuaded it would benefit students and could be integrated into the school's existing programs and structures. Rules, forms, and procedures were reviewed and modified as appropriate to support a schoolwide resilience-based approach. Mr. Caine became an advocate for the resiliency approach and often discussed this approach with other principals and district officials. Implementation of a resilience focus became established as a schoolwide goal.

Resources for Background Information on Resiliency

Benard, B. (1991, August). *Resiliency in kids: Protective factors in the family, school, and community.* Portland, OR: Northwest Regional Educational Laboratory.

Bosworth, K. (2000). *Protective schools: Linking drug abuse prevention with student success.* Tucson: University of Arizona.

Blum, R. W., McNeely, C. A., & Rinehart, P. M. (2002). *Improving the odds: The untapped power of schools to improve the health of teens.* Minneapolis: Center for Adolescent Health and Development, University of Minnesota.

Fullan, M. (1999). *Change forces: The sequel.* Philadelphia: Falmer Press.

Henderson, N., & Milstein, M. M. (1996). *Resiliency in schools: Making it happen for students and educators.* Thousand Oaks, CA: Corwin Press.

Katz, M. (1997). *On playing a poor hand well.* New York: W.W. Norton & Co.

Krovetz, M. L. (1999). *Fostering resiliency.* Thousand Oaks, CA: Corwin Press.

Oakley, E., & Krug, D. (1991). *Enlightened leadership.* New York: Fireside.

Rutter, M., Maughan, B., Martimore, P., & Ouston, J. (1979). *Fifteen thousand hours.* Cambridge, MA: Harvard University Press.

Scales, P. C., & Leffort, N. (1999). *Developmental assets: A synthesis of the scientific research on adolescent development.* Minneapolis, MN: Search Institute.

Werner, E. E., & Smith, R. S. (1982). *Vulnerable but invincible: A longitudinal study of resilient children and youth.* New York: McGraw-Hill.

Werner, E. E., & Smith, R. S. (1992). *Overcoming the odds: High-risk children from birth to adulthood.* Ithaca, NY: Cornell University.

During the third year, a systematic review of existing structural elements of the school was undertaken. Staff development was provided to assist teachers in implementing a resiliency direction. Following are some of the changes Jefferson made to support a resiliency approach.

1. Office referral forms were modified to have teachers identify a student's strengths as well as reasons for referral. The principal began returning the form to any teacher who failed to include strengths.
2. The school adopted an evidence-based school climate and violence prevention program that was implemented schoolwide. A key component of this program is an emphasis on a common language and abundant praise for positive behavior.
3. Regular schoolwide award assemblies were scheduled to recognize a variety of accomplishments.
4. Bulletin boards were installed in the hallways for continuous display of student work.
5. The counselor began writing a column for the parent newsletter about ways to promote resiliency in the home.

This past year a new principal (Arlene Feeney) was assigned to Jefferson. Although she had worked in the district for many years, she had limited familiarity with resiliency. Maria Telles and other committed staff members met with her several times to introduce the concepts to her. Ms. Feeney read several books and talked with school personnel. Because of their positive attitude toward the resilience approach and the numerous benefits they reported, she has continued the resilience focus at Jefferson. Resiliency has become the foundation for all school programs and practices. As Maria said at the end of the third year of implementation, "By changing the way people think about children, it will be impossible for this resiliency approach to evaporate."

Mountain Vista Middle School

In the mid 1990s, as the nation was in shock at a number of highly publicized school shootings, Mountain Vista was experiencing an increase in violent and aggressive incidents. Principal Jack Snyder had a vision of resiliency for his students: that they would have "skills beyond just their educational skills—skills to get along with people, skills to overcome problems and to work through problems." He described himself as a "poster child" for resiliency, having investigated the concept of resiliency over the years because it mirrored his own experience of being successful in spite of a troubled childhood. He felt it was his responsibility to make his school the same kind of safe haven that school had been for him when he was growing up. "The school and teachers saved my life," he recounted.

This commitment led him to assign new counselor Carrie Jimenez the responsibility of finding an appropriate violence prevention curriculum that would teach all students skills for conflict resolution and problem solving. Carrie had attended a conference on resiliency and began using that language in the school as she searched for an approach that would mesh with the school culture.

First, she created a short needs assessment survey for the staff to identify the most critical discipline and behavior issues. Nearly all the staff concurred with Mr. Snyder's observation that an excessive amount of time was spent on responding to inappropriate student behaviors and student conflicts. This input gave Carrie guidelines for her search. After reviewing the literature and visiting the Web sites of the U.S. Department of Education and the Substance Abuse and Mental Health Services Administration (SAMHSA), she identified two programs that fit with the needs identified by the Mountain Vista staff, only one of which was within the school's budget.

Carrie presented her findings to the faculty. After discussion, the faculty approved the adoption of the Second Step curriculum (Grossman et al., 1997), agreeing to implement the lessons in their classrooms. Mr. Snyder then arranged for Carrie to attend training sponsored by the curriculum development group and become certified as a Second Step trainer. In three sessions, Carrie trained the faculty and staff to implement the curriculum: Each teacher was responsible for teaching three components: empathy, problem solving, and anger management. The teachers were enthusiastic, so the program was implemented schoolwide over a full academic year, with Carrie providing support and coaching as needed. Mr. Snyder demonstrated his support by including the implementation of the curriculum and its principles as part of his classroom observations and teacher evaluations. Mr. Snyder and Carrie used the problem-solving steps of Second Step in student discipline conferences. Support staff, including playground monitors, were trained in the language and principles of the program, so a consistent message of violence prevention would pervade the school.

In the second year, the PTA contributed funds to provide booster sessions for the teachers and training for the parents. Signs displaying the problem-solving steps papered the hall and classroom walls to remind everyone of the new approach to problem solving and conflict resolution. Carrie was responsible for overseeing the implementation process. Throughout the first two years of implementation, teachers filled out quarterly progress reports on their individual classrooms. They identified the lessons they had taught, strategies that had worked well, and what additional resources and support they needed. Each month a portion of the faulty meeting was devoted to providing feedback on Second Step implementation. Faculty members freely discussed successes and problems, thus building a strong knowledge base about the program and its application in the classroom.

The counselor's role was that of coach and consultant. As such, she gathered feedback about classroom use of Second Step, facilitated staff discussions, and conducted booster sessions. Occasionally, at the request of the teacher, Carrie would observe or co-teach a lesson so she could provide direct feedback. Being aware that unless the curriculum was implemented as written, it would not have the intended impact, she monitored the fidelity with which the teachers implemented the lessons. Carrie avoided teaching many Second Step lessons herself from a belief that "the teachers needed not only to be teaching the material so they would know it, but also so they could practice the skills in their everyday interactions with children. There are hundreds of times during a week when a teacher can reinforce a lesson or skills from the curriculum."

At the end of two years, all teachers had implemented the majority of the lessons. The biggest impediment to implementation was the conflict with instructional time. On the other hand, Mr. Snyder identified a consistent reduction in disciplinary referrals and aggressive incidents, which he attributed to Second Step. The year before the curriculum was introduced, 227 incidents of aggression, fighting, or other violence had been reported to the office. That number fell to 177 in the first year of implementation and to 51 in the second year. Over the three years, he noted marked behavior changes in the students who had been exposed to several years of the curriculum.

After three years of implementation, both Mr. Snyder and Carrie left the school. Their replacements were briefed on Second Step and agreed to support its continued implementation. Although the teachers were encouraged to continue Second Step in their classrooms, no booster sessions or faculty meeting time was devoted to the issue.

Five years after the initial implementation, a survey of teachers who had been at the school since the implementation phase revealed that more than 86% were still using some Second Step lessons in their classrooms. Thus, even though the Second Step had not been formally supported for more than two years, the work that Carrie and Mr. Snyder did to build capacity in the teachers survived for several years.

The thoughtful implementation process used at Mountain Vista was key in sustaining the use of this effective violence prevention program. Here are the steps used in this implementation process:

1. Developing background knowledge of resiliency and violence prevention.
2. Ensuring commitment from leadership.
3. Developing an implementation plan.
4. Educating the faculty.
5. Involving the faculty in decision making.
6. Providing intense, high-quality initial training.
7. Scheduling coaching, follow-up, and booster sessions.
8. Monitoring progress and revising implementation when appropriate.
9. Using consistent concepts and vocabulary schoolwide.

Randall and Harris Elementary Schools

Randall and Harris elementary schools are located within a mile of each other in a suburban area within five miles of an urban center. Over the past decade, much of the original population of Irish and Italian immigrants has moved farther from the city. The new residents represent a diverse group of recent immigrants from South America, Jamaica, Eastern Europe, and Asia. More than 40 languages are spoken in these schools.

Four years ago, both schools volunteered to participate in an evaluation study of a promising violence prevention curriculum. Counselors Jim Downey at Randall Elementary School and Tammy Ikeda at Harris Elementary School became acquainted through the quarterly meetings of schools in the evaluation project. They both agreed that although the program being evaluated was effective, they would like to see the peace-building principles expanded beyond classroom activities.

That spring a former Randall student was killed in a daylight drive-by shooting. Several siblings and other relatives of the murdered student still attended Randall and Harris. The community was shocked, and the high school counselor called a meeting of all the counselors in that attendance area to discuss what could be done to respond to the community's grief and anger and to prevent more violence.

The counselors developed the idea of a peace march and conference. This activity would involve students at all three levels — elementary, middle, and high school—in a demonstration of support for peace and nonviolence. A visible symbol of all of the schools' commitment to nonviolence, the march would also attract positive press coverage about this community, which had had more than its share of negative publicity. The conference would include presentations, discussions, and skill-building sessions to support the violence prevention lessons being taught in school.

The counselors discussed the idea with their principals and received enthusiastic support. Jim volunteered to coordinate the Peace March and Tammy took leadership for the conference. Each worked with a planning team of counselors, teachers, and parents. Although initially enthusiastic, personnel at the other elementary schools, the middle school, and the high school gradually scaled back their participation. The bulk of the responsibility for planning came from the Harris and Randall schools, with support and resources from staff of the evaluation study.

On the day of the Peace March and Conference, third-, fourth-, and fifth-grade students from the Harris and Randall schools, as well as a few representatives of the other schools, met at a park between the two schools. The younger students participated in peace activities in their classrooms. The classes that met at the park had made banners with peace slogans on them. Several speakers addressed the group, then the students chose whether to participate in non-competitive games, peace artwork, or communication skills workshops. These sessions were led by high school students and parent volunteers. A local fast food company served lunch, after which the students returned to their respective schools.

All connected with the Peace March were pleased with the event and began planning another event for the following year. Although Tammy and Jim continued to play leadership roles, several enthusiastic community and parent volunteers emerged to share leadership responsibilities.

Although the evaluation project that had supported the inaugural Peace March and Conference terminated five years ago, the peace event has continued annually. Two years ago Jim retired, and last year Tammy became principal at an elementary school in a neighboring district. Their replacements at Harris and Randall have continued to plan the event with the enthusiastic support of their respective principals. The number of participating schools has expanded to include active participation of all schools in the attendance area, fulfilling the initial vision of involvement from students at all grade levels. Several nearby elementary schools have also joined in. As the number of schools increased to eight, it became unmanageable to include all students in the actual march and conference. Therefore, each school was asked to send 50 "peace ambassadors" to the event. Each school developed different strategies for selecting their ambassadors. Each school also was responsible for organizing peace-related activities at its local campus for those students who could not participate in the Peace March and Conference. Many schools duplicated the agenda from the first event and offered sessions in conflict resolution, peace art, and noncompetitive games. Frequently, parents and middle and high school students helped lead these sessions and other activities.

Tammy and Jim's leadership and organizational skills got the event off the ground and laid the foundation for it to become a community institution. Planning this event required organizational skills and communication skills, as well as an ability to mobilize volunteers. While Jim and Tammy initially had support from the evaluation team, over the second and third years, progressively more responsibility for planning and organizing the Peace March was shifted away from the paid evaluation staff to parent and community volunteers. At the end of the fifth year, parents and community volunteers formed a nonprofit corporation to continue the Peace March and Conference. Counselors continue to play important roles in the Peace March and Conference, but more of their time and energy is focused on planning the activities within their individual schools.

Lessons Learned

Although the counselor's role in each of these cases was different, some common themes can be identified. The lessons learned from the experiences in these very different schools can inform the implementation of a resiliency program in other schools or educational institutions. It is clear that counselors' skills in developing and maintaining relationships, researching, organizing, working with diverse groups, and persuading place them in an ideal position to move a resiliency agenda forward in a school.

The following eight lessons can be extracted from a review of the case studies:

1. The counselor independently sought opportunities to learn about resiliency, either through reading or attending a conference or workshop.
2. The counselor teamed up with the principal to plan and implement a resiliency approach. The counselor took the responsibility for educating the principal in resiliency principles.
3. Throughout the implementation phase, counselors served as teachers, guides, role models, and coaches for the faculty and staff.
4. Implementing the changes required careful planning.
5. The change process took several years.
6. Although the basic principles remained constant, the resiliency approach changed and grew over each year of implementation.
7. As with most successful implementations, relationships and organizational skills were key factors.
8. The concept of resiliency development was powerful enough to endure despite changes in administration and personnel. As with any program, however, booster sessions and additional training to keep skills updated were essential.

---

*With contributions from Mary Nebe and Cindy Hurley, counselors with the Tucson Unified School District, Tucson, AZ, and Steve Nagel, Tucson LINKS Training Coordinator, University of Arizona.

Figure 8.1. Resiliency in Your School
A teacher affects eternity; no one can tell where his influence stops.
– Henry Adams

What Is Resiliency?
• the ability to succeed in the face of adversity
• the process of self-righting and growth
• the capacity to meet challenges and become more capable
  as a result of these experiences

Six Key Factors That Foster Resiliency in Students

Factor	*Benefits to Students*
Pro-social bonding: connections with persons and activities that are healthy and supportive of positive growth	Students are less likely to engage in risk-related relationships and behaviors
Clear and consistent boundaries: defined and agreed-on expectations for behavior/consequences; enforced equitably	Leads to feelings of safety and freedom, and in turn, to more positive participation
Life skills: communication, problem-solving, decision-making, goal-setting, conflict resolution, and assertiveness skills	Skills required to navigate successfully through life
Caring and support: unconditional positive regard, trust, and love	Can lead to an increased sense of worth and value
High, supported expectations: achievement orientation that is based on abilities and potential, and provides motivation	High but realistic expectations support success
Meaningful participation: opportunities to become involved; help others; and engage in group problem solving, planning, and goal setting	Meaningful participation can promote belonging and connection

SOURCE: Henderson and Milstein (1996)

What Can Teachers Do to Foster Resiliency in Their Students?
• Practice and promote the six key factors listed in the table.
• Use a high-warmth, low-criticism style of interaction.
• Encourage goal setting and mastery.
• Appreciate the unique talents of each individual student.
• Promote sharing of responsibilities, service to others, and "required helpfulness."

What Are the Characteristics of Schools That Support Student Resiliency?
• Rewards and praise are used frequently and effectively.
• Surroundings are pleasant and comfortable—if not new, at least clean and well kept.
• Students are given responsibilities and encouraged to participate.
• The school community emphasizes academic effort.
• Positive role models exist throughout the school.
• Classrooms are efficiently managed.
• Positive and respectful relationships are nurtured among and between adults and students.

References

Alan Guttmacher Institute. (1999). *Facts in brief: Teen sex and pregnancy.* New York and Washington: Author. Available from: http://www.agi-usa.org/pubs/fb_teen_sex.pdf

American School Counselor Association. (2003). *The ASCA national model: A framework for school counseling programs.* Alexandria, VA: Author.

Bearman, P. S., Jones, J., & Udry, J. R. (1997). *National longitudinal study of adolescent health: Study design.* Available from: http://www.cpc.unc.edu/addhealth

Benard, B. (1991, August). *Resiliency in kids: Protective factors in the family, school, and community.* Portland, OR: Northwest Regional Educational Laboratory.

Benson, P. (1997, Winter). Connecting resiliency, youth development, and asset development in a positive-focused framework for youth. *Resiliency in Action, 2(1),* 19–22.

Bickart, T. B., & Wolin, S. J. (1997). Practicing resilience in the elementary classroom. *Principal, 77*(2). Available from: http://www.projectresilience.com/framespublications.htm

Blanchard, K., & Waghorn, T. (1997). *Mission possible.* New York: McGraw-Hill.

Blum, R. W., McNeely, C. A., & Rinehart, P. M. (2002). *Improving the odds: The untapped power of schools to improve the health of teens.* Minneapolis: Center for Adolescent Health and Development, University of Minnesota.

Borman, G. D., & Rachuba, L. T. (2001, February). *Academic success among poor and minority students: An analysis of competing models of school effects.* (Rep. No. 52) Baltimore, MD: Johns Hopkins University & Howard University Center for Research on Education of Students Placed At Risk.

Bosworth, K. (1995, May). Caring for others and being cared for: Students talk caring in school. *Phi Delta Kappan, 76*(9), 686–693.

Bosworth, K. (2000). *Protective Schools: Linking drug abuse prevention with student success.* Tucson: University of Arizona.

Bosworth, K., Gingiss, P. M., Pottoff, C., & Roberts-Gray, C. (1999). A Bayesian model to predict the success of the implementation of health and education innovations in school-centered programs. *Evaluation and Program Planning, 22,* 1–11.

Bowers, J. L., & Hatch, P. A. (2002). *The national model for school counseling programs.* Alexandria, VA: American School Counselor Association.

Bureau of Labor Statistics. (1998). *News: United States Department of Labor* (USDL Publication No. 98-253). Washington, DC: United States Government Printing Office.

Campbell, P. H., Milbourne, S. A., & Silverman, C. (2001). Strength-based child portfolios: A professional development activity to alter perspectives of children with special needs. *Topics in Early Childhood Special Education, 21*(3), 152–161.

Career Action Center. (1996). *Principles underlying career self reliance.* No location indicated. Author.

Carr, E. G., Horner, R. H., Turnbull, A. P., Marquis, J. G., McLaughlin, D. M., McAtee, M. L., Smith, C. E., Ryan, K. A., Ruef, M. B., Doolabh, A., & Braddock, D. (1999). *Positive behavior support for people with developmental disabilities: A research synthesis.* Washington, DC: American Association on Mental Retardation.

Centers for Disease Control and Prevention. (2000, June 9). CDC surveillance summaries. *Morbidity and Mortality Weekly Report, 49*(SS-5). Available from: http://www.cdc.gov/mmwr/PDF/SS/SS4905.pdf

Centers for Disease Control and Prevention. (2001). *Youth risk behavior surveillance system. 2001 information and results.* Available from: http://www.cdc.gov/HealthyYouth/yrbs/data/2001/index.html

Chatzky, (2003, May 23–25). *USA Weekend,* 4.

Clark, M. D. (1998, June). Strength-based practice: The ABC's of working with adolescents who don't want to work with you. *Federal Probation, 62*(1), 46–53.

Collard, B., Epperheimer, J. W., & Saign, D. (1996). *Career resilience in a changing workplace.* Columbus, OH: ERIC Clearinghouse on Adult, Career, and Vocational Education. (ERIC Document Reproduction Service No. ED396191)

Dawis, R. V., England, G. W., & Lofquist, L. H. (1964). A theory of work adjustment. *Minnesota Studies in Vocational Rehabilitation, XV,* 1–27.

Deevy, E. (1995). *Creating the resilient organization: A rapid response management program.* Englewood Cliffs, NJ: Prentice Hall.

DeJong, W., & Moegkens, B. A. (1995). *Institutionalizing an alcohol and other drug prevention program* (Publication No. ED/OPE95-10). Newton, VA: Higher Education Center for Alcohol and Other Drug Prevention. Available from: http://www.edc.org/hec/pubs/institut.htm

Developmental Studies Center. (2002). *Ways we want our class to be.* Oakland, CA: Author.

Farrington, D. P. (1989). Early predictors of adolescent aggression and adult violence. *Violence and Victims, 4,* 79–100.

Feller, R., & Whichard, J. (2005). *Knowledge nomads and the nervously employed: Workplace change and courageous career choices.* Austin, TX: ProEd.

Felner, R. D., Favazza, A., Shim, M., Brand, S., Gu, K., & Noonan, N. (2001). Whole school improvement and restructuring and prevention and promotion. *Journal of School Psychology, 39*(2), 177–202.

Fullan, M. (1999). *Change forces: The sequel.* Philadelphia: Falmer Press.

Gardner, H. (1993). *Multiple intelligences.* New York: Basic Books.

Gelatt, H. B. (1991). *Creative decision making: Using positive uncertainty.* Los Altos, CA: Crisp.

Gelatt, H. B. (1998). Self, system, synergy: A career–life development framework for individuals and organizations. *Career Planning and Adult Development Journal, 14*(3),13–23.

Goldberg, B., Frost-Pineda, K., & Gold, M. (2002). Ecstasy deaths in the state of Florida: A post-mortem analysis. *Biological Psychology, 51*(8), 192–97.

Goleman, D. (1995). *Emotional intelligence.* New York: Bantam Books.

Gottfredson, D. C., Gottfredson, G. D., & Skroban, S. B. (1996). A multimodal school-based prevention demonstration. *Journal of Adolescent Research, 11*(1), 97–115.

Grant, B. F., & Dawson, D. A. (1997). Age at onset of alcohol use and its association with *DSM-IV* alcohol abuse and dependence: Results from the national longitudinal alcohol epidemiological survey. *NIAAA Journal of Substance Abuse, 9,* 103–110.

Griffith, C. (1998). Building a resilient workforce. *Training, 35,* 1, 54–56, 58, 60.

Grossman, D. C., Neckerman, J. J., Koepsell, T.D., Liu, P., Asher, K. N., Beland, K., Frey, K., & Rivara, F. P. (1997). Effectiveness of a violence prevention curriculum among children in elementary school: A randomized trial. *Journal of the American Medical Association, 277,* 1605–1611.

Grzeda, M. M. (1999). Reconceptualizing career change: A career development perspective. *Career Development International, 4*(6), 305–11.

Gysbers, N. C., & Henderson, P. (1997). *Comprehensive guidance programs that work—II.* Greensboro, NC: ERIC/CASS Publications.

Gysbers, N. C., & Moore, E. J. (1974). *Career guidance, counseling, and placement: Elements of an illustrative program guide (A life career development perspective).* Columbia, MO: University of Missouri, Columbia.

Hawkins J. D., Catalano, R. F., & Miller, J. Y. (1992). Risk and protective factors for alcohol and other drug problems in adolescence and early adulthood: Implications for substance abuse prevention. *Psychological Bulletin, 112*(1), 64–105.

Henderson, N., & Milstein, M. M. (1996). *Resiliency in schools: Making it happen for students and educators.* Thousand Oaks, CA: Corwin Press.

Herr, E. L. (1992). Counseling for personal flexibility in a global economy. *Educational and Vocational Guidance, 53*, 5–16.

Holland, J. L. (1959). A theory of vocational choice. *Journal of Counseling Psychology, 6*, 35–45.

Ivey, A., & Goncalves, O. F. (1988). Developmental theory: Integrating developmental processes into clinical practice. *Journal of Counseling & Development, 66*(9), 406–413.

Janas, M. (2002). Build resiliency. *Intervention in School and Clinic, 38*(2), 117–121.

Johnson, S. (1998). *Who moved my cheese?* New York: G. P. Putnam's Sons.

Johnston, L. D., O'Malley, P. M., & Bachman, J. G. (2003). *Monitoring the future national survey results on drug use, 1975–2002. Vol. I: Secondary school students* (NIH Publication No. 03-5375). Bethesda, MD: National Institute on Drug Abuse.

Kaiser Family Foundation. (2003). *National survey of adolescents and young adults: Sexual health knowledge, attitudes, and experiences.* (Publication No. 3218). Menlo Park, CA: Author. Available from:http://www.kff.org/youthhivstats/loader.cfm?url=/commonspot/security/getfile.cfm&PageID=14269

Katz, M. (1997). *On playing a poor hand well.* New York: W.W. Norton & Co.

Kelder, S. H., Orpinas, P., McAlister, A., Frankowski, R., Parcel, G. S., & Friday, J. (1996). Youth violence prevention: Descriptions and baseline data from 13 evaluation projects. *American Journal of Preventive Medicine, 12*(Suppl. 5), 22–39.

Kellam, S. G., Ling, X., Merisca, R., Brown, C. H., & Ialongo, N. (1998). Effects of the level of aggression in the first-grade classroom on the course and malleability of aggressive behavior into middle school. *Development and Psychopathology, 10,* 165–185.

Krovetz, M. L. (1999). *Fostering resiliency.* Thousand Oaks, CA: Corwin Press.

Lieber, C. M., & Civitas, J. R. (1994). Challenging beliefs and bureaucracies in an urban school system. *Education & Urban Society, 27*(4), 25–70.

Lloyd, C. (1997). *Creating a life worth living: A practical course in career decision making for artists, innovators, and others aspiring to a creative life.* New York: Harper Collins.

London, M. (1998). *Career barriers: How people experience, overcome, and avoid failure.* Mahwah, NJ: Lawerence Erlbaum.

Martin, P. J. (2002). Transforming school counseling: A national perspective. *Theory Into Practice, 27*(3), 149–153.

Michigan Department of Career Development. (2002). *Adventures in career pathways.* Lansing, MI: Author.

Mitchell, K. E., Levin, A. L., & Krumboltz, J. D. (1999). Planned happenstance: Constructing unexpected career opportunities. *Journal of Counseling & Development, 2,* 115–124.

Moren, S. F., & Collins, C. (2000). Substance abuse prevention: Moving from science to policy. *Addictive Behaviors, 25*(6), 975–983.

Myrick, R. D. (1987). *Developmental guidance and counseling: A practical approach.* Minneapolis, MN: Educational Media Corporation.

Nadel, H., Spellman, M., & Alvarez-Canino, T. (1996). The cycle of violence and victimization: A study of the school-based intervention of a multidisciplinary youth violence prevention program. *Youth Violence Prevention, 12*(5), 109–119.

National Association of Secondary School Principals. (1996). Breaking ranks: Changing an American institution. *NASSP Bulletin, 80*(578), 54–66.

National Center for Education Statistics. (2003). *Digest of education statistics, 2002.* Washington, DC: U.S. Department of Education.

Nickols, F. (2000). *Change management 101.* Available from: http://home.att.net/~nickols/change.htm

Noddings, N. (1992). *The challenge to care in schools: An alternative approach to education.* New York: Teachers College Press.

Noonan, C. (1999). Brief interventions foster student resiliency. *The Education Digest, 64*(8), 36–39.

Novick, R. (1998). The comfort corner: Fostering resilience and emotional intelligence. *Childhood Education, 74*(4), 200–204.

Oakley, E., & Krug, D. (1991). *Enlightened leadership.* New York: Fireside.

Peterson, J. V., & Nisenholz, B. (1999). *Orientation to counseling* (4th ed.). Boston: Allyn & Bacon.

Peterson, L. (1995). *Starting out, starting over.* Palo Alto, CA: Davies-Black.

Pope, M., & Minor, C. W. (2000). *Experiential activities for teaching career counseling classes and for facilitating career groups, Vol. 1.* Tulsa, OK: National Career Development Association.

Quinn, D., Greunert, S., & Valentine, J. (1999). *Using data for school improvement* (National Alliance of Middle Schools Monograph). Reston, VA: National Association of Secondary School Principals.

Rogers, E. M. (1995). *Diffusion of innovations* (4th ed.). New York: Free Press.

Rutter, M., Maughan, B., Martimore, P., & Ouston, J. (1979). *Fifteen thousand hours: Secondary schools and their effects on children.* Cambridge, MA: Harvard University Press.

Scales, P. C., & Leffort, N. (1999). *Developmental assets: A synthesis of the scientific research on adolescent development.* Minneapolis, MN: Search Institute.

Schlossberg, N. K., & Robinson, S. P. (1996). *Going to Plan B.* New York: Simon & Schuster.

Schlossberg, N. K., Waters, E. B., & Goodman, J. (1995). *Counseling adults in transition.* New York: Springer.

Schwann, C. J., & Spady, W. G. (1998). *Total leaders.* Arlington, VA: American Association of School Administrators.

Seligman, M. E. P. (1998). *Learned optimism* (2nd. ed.). New York: Pocket Books.

Stevens, P. (2001). *Bottoms up succession planning works better.* Sydney, Australia: Center for Worklife Counseling.

Stone, C. B., & Clark, M. A. (2001, April). School counselors and principals: Partners in support of academic achievement. *NASSP Bulletin, 85*(624), 47–53.

Substance Abuse and Mental Health Services Administration. (2002). *Results from the 2001 National Household Survey on Drug Abuse: Volume I. Summary of National Findings* (Office of Applied Studies, NHSDA Series H-17, DHHS Publication No. SMA 02-3758). Rockville, MD: Author.

Sugai, G., Horner, R. H., Dunlap, G., Hieneman, M., Lewis, T. J., Nelson, C. M., Scott, T., Liaupsin, C., Sailor, W., Turnbull, A. P., Turnbull, H. R. III., Wickham, D., Ruef, M., & Wilcox, B. (2000). Applying positive behavioral supports and functional behavioral assessment in schools. *Journal of Positive Behavior Interventions, 2*(3), 131–144.

Sullivan, C. (2003). A bakers' dozen of career counseling activities — part deux. Rochester, MI: Class presentation, June 3.

Swisher, J. D. (2000). Sustainability of prevention. *Addictive Behaviors, 25*(6), 965–973.

Taylor, L., & Adelman, H. S. (2000, June). Connecting schools, families, and communities. *ASCA Professional School Counseling, 3*(5), 298–307.

Ventura, S. J., Mosher, W. D., Curtin, S. C., Abma, J. C., & Henshaw, S. (1999). Highlights of trends in pregnancies and pregnancy rates by outcome: Estimates for the United States, 1976–1996. *National Vital Statistics Reports, 47*(29). Available from: http://www.cdc.gov/nchs/data/nvsr/nvsr47/nvs47_29.pdf

Wakefield, S. M., Sage, H., Coy, D. R., & Palmer, T. (Eds.). (2004). *Unfocused kids: Helping students to focus on their education and career plans.* Greensboro, NC: CAPS Press.

Werner, E. (1999). How children become resilient: Observations and cautions. In N. Henderson, B. Benard, & N. Sharp-Light (Eds.), *Resiliency in action: Practical ideas for overcoming risks and building strengths in youth, families, & communities.* Goreham, ME: Resiliency in Action.

Werner, E. E., & Smith, R. S. (1982). *Vulnerable but invincible: A longitudinal study of resilient children and youth.* New York: McGraw-Hill.

Werner, E. E., & Smith, R. S. (1992). *Overcoming the odds: High-risk children from birth to adulthood.* Ithaca, NY: Cornell University Press.

Werner, E. E., & Smith, R. S. (2001). *Journeys from childhood to midlife: Risk, resilience, and recovery.* Ithaca, NY: Cornell University Press.

Wheatley, M. J. (1999). *Leadership and the new science: Discovering order in a chaotic world.* San Francisco: Berrett-Koehler.

Wheatley, M. J., & Kellner-Rogers, M. (1998, April–May). Bringing life to organizational change. *Journal of Strategic Performance Measurement, 5,* 13.

Wiist, H., Jackson, R. H., and Jackson, K. W. (1996). The cycle of violence and victimization: A study of the school-based intervention of a multidisciplinary youth violence prevention program. *Youth Violence Prevention, 12*(5), 56–64.

Zimmerman, J. (1994, May). Resiliency versus risk: Helping kids help themselves. *Far West Laboratory Focus on Changing School Practice, 1,* 4.

DATE DUE